THE
GHOST

The Murder of Police Chief Greg Adams and the Hunt for His Killer

D1521273

THE GHOST

The Murder of Police Chief Greg Adams
and the Hunt for His Killer

MAUREEN BOYLE

Black Lyon Publishing, LLC

THE GHOST:
The Murder of Police Chief Greg Adams
and the Hunt for his Killer

Copyright © 2021 by Maureen Boyle

All rights reserved.

No part of this book may be used or reproduced in any way
by any means without the written permission of the publisher,
except in the case of brief quotations embodied in critical articles
and reviews.

Please note that if you have purchased this book without a cover
or in any way marked as an advance reading copy, you have
purchased a stolen item, and neither the author nor the publisher
has been compensated for their work.

This is a work of non-fiction. All direct quotes are either from
recorded interviews, interviews with individuals by local
media at the time or the recollection of the individuals during
interviews with the author of what was said at the time. When
possible, those interviewed reviewed their recollected quotes for
accuracy.

Our books may be ordered through your local bookstore or by
visiting the publisher:

www.BlackLyonPublishing.com

Black Lyon Publishing, LLC
PO Box 567
Baker City, OR 97814

ISBN: 978-1-934912-96-6
Library of Congress Control Number: 2021937169

Published and printed in the United States of America.

Black Lyon True Crime

Praise for this book

"Gripping! Incredible storytelling. Maureen has a way of taking you through every moment of this real-life drama. A story told with compassionate truth, and dazzling detail."

— Jerry Penacoli, former host of *EXTRA*

"Maureen Boyle's journalism experience shines in her impeccably researched books--and her storytelling skills are stellar!"

—Hank Phillippi Ryan *USA Today* Bestselling Author

"The author of Shallow Graves does it again. With the trained eye of a seasoned police reporter, Maureen Boyle gathers the pertinent facts, amassing details and connecting the dots as she chronicles the search for a cop killer with mob ties and many aliases who eluded the law for decades. The Ghost is another meticulous work of true-crime narrative nonfiction from a journalist who always gets it right. The Ghost is a haunting story of justice delayed but never forgotten."

—Irene Virag, Pulitzer Prize-winning reporter and Assistant Dean at Stony Brook University

"Maureen Boyle is everything a true crime writer should be. Tenacious. Unrelenting. And empathetic. Her new book The Ghost *examines the nationwide manhunt for a low-level wannabe mobster on the run from the longest cold case murder in history—the brutal execution of a young police officer in a tiny Pennsylvania town. It is a riveting thriller that takes us on this chase for the man the FBI called a 'flashy dresser, a lover of dogs, and a big tipper.' I cannot recommend it enough."*

—Michele McPhee, author of
Mayhem, A Mob Story, When Evil Rules

More praise for this book

"It may seem the work of fiction that a career criminal, having committed a notorious murder and under pursuit by multiple police agencies, could simply disappear. Yet it happened, and Maureen Boyle's compelling narrative of this real-life "ghost," and the close calls and frustrations of police who so badly wanted to nab him, will keep you reading as you, too, wonder how one can apparently vanish from the earth. This engrossing book, all true, will make you feel as if you are yourself part of the chase. Buckle up."

—Gary Craig, author
Seven Million: A Cop, a Priest, a Soldier for the IRA
and *The Still Unsolved Rochester Brink's Heist*

"Meticulously reported and beautifully written, with tragic characters and bizarre plot twists that would be hard to believe if they weren't real. Once again, Maureen Boyle's superb journalistic skills have produced a gripping and unforgettable true-crime story that you won't be able to put down."

—Elaine McArdle, co-author of
The Neuroscientist Who Lost Her Mind, The Migraine Brain
and senior editor at *UU World* magazine

"Boyle once again demonstrates her gifts for meticulous reporting and gripping narrative while never losing sight of the real human lives and emotions at stake. Ghost is as compelling—and cautionary—as true-crime gets."

—Chris Gonsalves, author of *Haunted Love*

Dedication

*To the memory of Chief Gregory B. Adams
and all the law enforcement officers killed yearly.*

Chapter 1
The Killing

From inside the Freehling home, windows closed against the December cold, 17-year-old Donald "Tiger" Freehling heard the slightly muffled sound.

It sounded like someone was hitting a stick against a tree.

Then he heard a loud boom.

The teen, home sick from school, looked out his second floor bedroom window. His family lived two houses up from the local Agway store, and just a few blocks from downtown and the police station. It was generally a quiet area in the semi-rural community of Saxonburg, Pennsylvania, population roughly 1,300.

He thought he could hear a faint cry for help but he couldn't see anyone.

He yelled to his mother, Midge Freehling, who was vacuuming the living room rug downstairs.

"Someone is calling for help outside," he said.

"Quit fooling around," she answered.

Butler Street, where the Freehling family lived across from the town cemetery, was a fairly quiet area. The biggest issue was the occasional speeder stopped by the town's Police Chief for driving over the 25 mile per hour speed limit.

The two peered out another window in the house and spotted what looked like a man, facedown in the snow near the hedges of their house, not far from the Agway feed store.

Midge could now hear a voice.

"Help me. Help me."

She slowly stepped outside into the snow. Who was this man? Why was he here?

She saw blood near the man's body. She inched closer. He was wearing a uniform. A police officer's uniform. She leaned down and rolled him over. She knew him.

It was Greg Adams, the town's Police Chief.

"I've been shot. I've been shot," he whispered to her. "I'm shot in the stomach."

She looked at his shirt. There was blood. So much blood.

She told him to lay still and not move.

"Don't worry, Greg, you're going to be all right."

She hovered over him, struggling to keep him still, hoping somehow to stop the bleeding.

"Who did it? Who did it?" She kept asking.

"A man," he answered.

"Who?"

"I don't know. I stopped his car. He took my gun."

Midge kept pressure on the wounds and kept talking.

"Hang on. Hang on. It's going to be okay. Hang on. Help is coming."

"I'm not going to make it," he told her. "Pray for me."

She ordered her son to run back into the house and call the police.

From the distance, she could hear the fire whistle then the fire department ambulance siren nearing. She caught the glimpse of a white car pulling out of the Agway Feed parking lot.

Brian Antoszyk, a volunteer firefighter and Emergency Medical Technician, first heard the call for an ambulance on the fire department radio at his home about a mile and a quarter from the Agway store. Then came the call on his pager. He hopped into his F250 pickup and started toward the station to pick up the ambulance.

When he was less than an eighth of a mile from the store,

the next call came through. It was a shooting. Brian drove right to the Agway.

He could see a person laying in the yard, and ran over. He couldn't tell who it was. As he got closer, all he could see were gray pants and a white T-shirt. He knelt next to the man to check on him.

"Brian," the man said.

He recognized the voice. It was his friend, Police Chief Greg Adams.

"Brian, this is bad," he heard the Chief say. "This is bad."

Brian looked closely at the Chief's bloodied and battered face. He couldn't recognize his friend.

"No, you are okay," Brian answered. "You are okay. You will be okay."

Brian glanced around the yard. He could trace the fierce battle for life where the frozen grass reached through the dusting of snow. The Chief's uniform shirt had been torn off and was laying in the yard.

"This is bad. This is bad," the Chief repeated.

And then he mentioned his boys and his wife. "I'm not going to be there," he said.

"Don't worry about it," Brian answered. "You will be. You will be."

As the ambulance pulled up, Brian prayed he would be right.

At the sound of the fire whistle three miles away, the alert for the town's volunteer firefighters, Gordon Mainhart turned to his newlywed wife, Cindy.

"Got to go, that's the fire call," he told her as he headed to his blue Mustang parked outside their house. It was officially his day off as one of the town's two full-time police officers. But, like many in semi-rural communities in western Pennsylvania in 1980, Gordon wore several public service hats. In addition to being a police officer, he was one of the more than a dozen volunteer firefighters, and was an Emergency Medical Technician, sometimes driving the ambulance to the hospital in nearby Butler nearly a half hour away.

That fire whistle was the call to action

Halfway up Main Street, heading to the fire station, Harriet Lassinger—who dispatched the fire and ambulance calls—was flagging him down.

"There's been a shooting at the Agway parking lot," she told him. "They think Greg's been shot."

Gordon floored his car.

Glenn Fair, also a volunteer firefighter and Emergency Medical Technician, was working on his car when the fire siren blew. He and his wife were renting an apartment atop the garage housing the town's ambulance and he was often one of the first at the scene in an emergency. The initial information on the scanner was vague: A man injured by the Agway. Then more specific: Possible gunshot victim. Within two minutes, he was pulling the ambulance out of the garage. Less than two minutes after that, he was in the backyard of the Freehling home with two other volunteer firefighters.

He could see Greg Adams, the town's 31-year-old Police Chief, on the ground and Brian Antoszyk next to him. There was a lot of blood.

Officer Gordon Mainhart had just pulled up and was running toward them.

"Greg, Greg, what happened? What happened? Do you know who did this? Who did this?" Gordon asked, leaning down.

"I don't know. I don't know," the Chief answered softly.

The officer dashed to the Chief's police cruiser. The car door was open. The microphone for the public address system was yanked out. Gordon grabbed the police radio mic.

"Officer down. Officer down. Shot. We're heading to Butler Hospital. We need an escort," he radioed, as his colleagues loaded the Chief into the ambulance.

Gordon turned and hopped into the rear of the ambulance with the Chief and fellow EMT/firefighter Charles Gamble.

The two cut his shirt off and kept pressure on what appeared to be two gunshot wounds as the ambulance sped off. The Chief wasn't wearing a bulletproof vest that day.

The equipment in the box-like ambulance used by the Saxonburg Fire Department was basic. There were bandages, lots of them. There was nothing to jolt a stopped heart. There was no heart monitor. Gordon would later call it a Band-Aid box on wheels. There was just Gordon and Charlie Gamble, another EMT, in the back, trying to keep the wounds closed, praying they could get to the hospital quick enough.

Driving at speeds reaching 80 miles per hour, Glenn Fair struggled to keep the vehicle on the icy road. Chuck Blakeley, another EMT in the front seat, gripped the dashboard and looked ashen.

"Go faster. Go faster," Gordon yelled from the rear.

Glenn kept his eyes on the road and said a silent prayer. *Let's get there in time.*

Gordon and Charlie kept pressure on the wound. "Hang in there. Hang in there," Gordon repeated. "We're almost there. Who did this? Who did this?"

The Chief began to close his eyes. "It burns. It burns. It burns," he answered.

The ambulance swayed on the icy road. Glenn let up on the gas, then accelerated. Butler Memorial Hospital was ten miles and close to 30 minutes from the Agway in Saxonburg in the winter. He needed to beat that time.

Each second counted.

The Pennsylvania state troopers were milling around the lobby in the Saxonburg municipal building on West Main Street, waiting for their cases to be called the afternoon of December 4, 1980. Just a few minutes earlier, Sue Haggerty, the administrative assistant, heard the distinctive "slish, slish" of the Police Chief's heels in the hallway, heading to the office. She could always tell when he was walking down the hall.

The Saxonburg Police Department was in the rear of the town's main municipal building, and the court offices to the front.

Chief Greg Adams often stopped in to drop off paperwork. This day was no different. Sue and the Chief likely exchanged a few pleasantries that afternoon. They likely talked about Christmas, just three weeks away. She thinks they talked a little bit about vacations. Nothing memorable. The Chief ran on the quiet side, always professional and business-like. He wasn't a sit-and-have-a-coffee kind of guy. Sue would later say she wished she could remember more of the conversation that day, maybe spent a few extra minutes chatting. But there was nothing special about those times when the Chief popped into the court office. It was just part of a routine day.

Shortly after three o'clock, about an hour or so after the Chief left, Sue heard the crackling call on the police radios carried by the troopers waiting to be called for court. So did everyone in the court offices. It was 3:02 p.m.

The Chief was shot in the parking lot at Agway, the local feed and garden product store, about 200 yards away.

Every police officer ran out the door.

Mary Ann Adams was in bed, her seven-month-old son asleep in his crib. It was shortly before 3:30 in the afternoon, and she was feeling the lingering effects of an infection. In a few weeks, her oldest son Ben would turn three the day before Christmas. She was trying to get as much rest as possible to get ready for the holidays. They were still deciding whether to head to Maryland, where her eldest sister and mother now lived, or celebrate at home. Either way, she wanted to get better and quickly.

Greg was at work, but was always just minutes from home. And when he was at home, he was always just minutes from work. That was the beauty of living and working in a small town like Saxonburg. However, the job was also all-encompassing.

When Greg wasn't on patrol, he would field phone calls from residents—or would head out to help at fires as one of the many volunteer firefighters.

Mary Ann knew from the start that Greg was a small town boy at heart. She'd met him on a packed bus to Maryland more than five years earlier when she was visiting her sister, hoping to find a job. There was just one seat left … next to him.

Mary Ann considered herself a shy and quiet young woman, not one to start up conversations with strangers. She had a book to read for the trip to occupy her and planned to ignore the man next to her. But Greg wanted to talk. And he did. For the entire trip.

She learned he was from the unincorporated community of Natrona Heights, Pennsylvania, about 25 miles from where she lived with her parents in the city of McKeesport. He was a police officer in Washington, D.C. on the Metropolitan Police Department but wanted to return to the quieter—and safer—lifestyle in Western Pennsylvania where his parents lived. He felt unsettled in the city.

By the time the bus pulled up to the terminal, Greg asked if they could go out while she was in the area. Mary Ann's heart sank. She didn't have her sister's address or phone number to give him. Her brother-in-law was picking her up at the station, so Greg waited at the station—then asked her brother-in-law, Louis Yoezle, if it was okay if he went out with Mary Ann. Her brother-in-law looked at her and smiled.

"Go for it," he told her.

Mary Ann never got a job in Maryland and eventually returned to her parents' home, but the move back to Pennsylvania seemed to only strengthen the new relationship between Mary Ann and Greg. He would often travel back to Pennsylvania to see her. He told her he wanted to leave Washington. The streets were too dangerous. Too many guns. Too much violence.

Between 1969 and the time he left the Washington force in early 1973, eight police officers had been killed in his department. He told Mary Ann he knew one of those officers.

During his time in Washington, Greg had gone undercover for drug investigations and was tiring of that street work. When he eventually spent a month teaching in the training academy, he found he loved it. But even with that brief change on the job, the Washington lifestyle and the rough streets were not to the liking of the Pennsylvania native. When he was passed over for a promotion, and his relationship with Mary Ann deepened, he began looking for work closer to his roots.

A year or so after the two met, he found a job on the Saxonburg Police Department in 1973 as an officer at a fraction of his previous salary. He and Mary Ann married in August of 1976.

From the start, Greg tried to keep even the symbols of the harder edges of police life from his wife. When they went on their honeymoon, Greg was careful to keep the personal handgun he often carried hidden. He hid it at the bottom of the trashcan in their room—then later discovered the maid tossed it out accidentally. He wasn't happy.

When Greg returned to Pennsylvania, he also renewed his love of teaching at the regional police academy where he stressed safety to the new officers. Always be on the alert. Never let your guard down. Wear your bulletproof vest. Remember: There are no routine calls.

Saxonburg—the job, the lifestyle, the people—seemed the perfect fit for Greg. It combined his love for law enforcement with his greater love for small, tight-knit communities.

As Mary Ann rested in bed the afternoon of December 4, 1980, she considered herself lucky. She was living in a safe town with two beautiful sons and a kind, loving husband. This was a wonderful life.

Then the phone in the living room rang. It was the local borough secretary, Ann Putz, on the other end.

"Mary Ann, are you listening to the scanner?"

"No."

"You need to get to the hospital right now. Greg's been shot. I'm coming to pick you up," Ann told her.

It took Mary Ann a minute to comprehend what her friend was saying. Shot? In Saxonburg? It must be an accident. Greg would probably be home that night or the next day, nursing a leg or arm wound, she thought.

Within five minutes, a neighbor who often babysat was at the house to watch the boys and her friend was at the door, urging Mary Ann to hurry up, they needed to get to the hospital.

Mary Ann tried to keep a single thought out of her mind: *This is not good.*

It took seven minutes to make what was normally a half-hour winter drive to Butler Memorial Hospital. The ambulance beat the police escort there. Gordon looked down at the Chief shortly before the ambulance pulled to the emergency room entrance. Greg had closed his eyes. He was lying still, too still, on the stretcher.

"Hang in there. Hang in there. We're at the hospital," Gordon repeated. "Hang in there."

The medical team was at the emergency room door to greet the ambulance and whisked the Chief inside.

Gordon and the three men in the ambulance stayed in the waiting room entryway. They each said a silent prayer. *Let him live.*

Gordon saw Mary Ann bolt into the hospital, gave her a hug, then stepped aside as the doctors escorted her to another room. Pennsylvania State Police officers were there to talk with her.

The emergency room doctor came out to the waiting area and slowly approached Gordon.

"There was nothing we could do," the doctor told him. "Even if he was shot in the hospital parking lot, we wouldn't have been able to save him."

Gordon took a deep breath and, with an anguished cry, punched the wall.

The two Pennsylvania state troopers in the waiting room with Mary Ann were somber.

"We're so sorry," one told her.

Mary Ann stood still. Her face turned pale.

I can't be a widow, she thought. *I can't be a widow. I can't be. We have two little boys. This can't be.*

The troopers paused. "We need to ask a few questions. It is important," they told her. "Did Greg have a second, non-service weapon? Did he have a second gun in the cruiser?"

"No," she told them. His only other handgun went missing during their honeymoon. His only handgun was his service weapon.

She would say later she couldn't remember if the troopers told her the circumstances of the shooting. She couldn't remember if they described the killer. She only knew one thing: Greg was dead and she had two children to raise alone. This was her new life.

Trooper Danny McKnight was running radar on Route 356, just south of Saxonburg, when the call came through. Officer shot. Be on the lookout for a white car, possibly a Cougar. He repositioned his cruiser to take up a position where he could easily see — and possibly chase — the car if it came by him.

And then he waited and watched, as did other police officers on the road throughout the area.

Troopers Jim Poydence and John Crede were on Route 38 north of Butler to serve a search warrant when the call came through on the radio. Officer shot in Saxonburg.

Jim turned to his partner. "That has to be Greg," he said. "He's on day shift this week."

They began driving quickly toward Saxonburg when the next call came through. The officer was dead on arrival at the hospital.

Two Pennsylvania State Police helicopters lifted off from a nearby airport, the airborne troopers inside hoping to catch a glimpse of the suspect's white car, possibly a Cougar. From the ground, residents like John Francis Rhyshek could hear the whirl of the 'copters overhead as they drove home and tuned on the radio news.

At the Butler State Police barracks, Jim Poydence's immediate supervisor, Corporal Richard Piccio, was already en route to the scene. He — and others — beat Jim and his partner there.

When Jim Poydence pulled up to the Agway, he could see the bustle of activity. Every cop was doing something: searching, documenting footprints, documenting where blood from the struggle fell.

Jim approached his boss. The corporal turned to Jim. "This is your case."

Jim took out a notebook and went to work.

The driver's side door of the Chief's cruiser was open. There was a clipboard on the seat. It appeared a piece of paper had been ripped away.

There were shell casings in the area. There was blood in the car.

The Chief's Smith & Wesson six-inch blue revolver, model 14-3, was gone. They would later learn it likely was fired at least twice. Another gun was found in the mud, a Colt .25 caliber automatic manufactured in October 1916. A chrome plate covered the original gun's metal blue.

The Chief's tie was on the cruiser trunk, apparently placed there by the woman who tried to help him.

The Chief's cruiser was facing inward in the parking lot. It appeared, based on tire tracks, the killer's car had been facing him.

A New Jersey driver's license with the name Stanley Portas of Phillipsburg, New Jersey, was found on the ground near the cruiser.

There was, they would later learn, Type O blood on the driver's door of the cruiser, the steering wheel, the Chief's gloves, the Chief's jacket. There was an "S" shaped trail of blood from the cruiser to where another car had been stopped. There was blood in the snow behind the Freehling house: Type A blood, the same blood type as the Chief, and more Type O, believed to be that of his killer.

Bullets were dug out of a maple tree the next day. A single bullet was dug out of the solid rubber full-width mud flap under the rear bumper of a pickup truck in the backyard of a house between the Agway and Freehling home. FBI agent Peter McCann found another as he walked the area with State Police Major Earl Wright. It was there on the ground, in the parking lot of Fox Funeral home, southwest of the shooting scene.

Jim and other investigators began to talk with neighbors, motorists and people inside the store. They began to piece together the fatal encounter. An elderly woman sitting in the front room of her house knitting, the window overlooking Agway across the street, saw a white car and a police cruiser pull into the business parking lot. Then she saw the white car leave.

Police surmised the Chief had passed the Agway after spotting a suspicious vehicle run a stop sign, turned around and saw the car in the parking lot. The Chief pulled in, his cruiser facing the suspect.

He didn't call in the stop. No one was sure why. No one saw the confrontation. No one knew exactly how it started, how it escalated. Did it happen quickly? Was the Chief trying to call in the license? Investigators later theorized he saw something suspicious in the car, was disarmed, was marched from the lot at gunpoint and then was struck in the back of the head.

The evidence—the blood specifically—showed there was a vicious struggle in the parking lot and behind two houses next door along Butler Street. The Chief was pistol-whipped. He was beaten. He was shot. An autopsy would later find he was shot twice—once in the armpit and once in the chest. The coroner, William F. Young Jr., later told reporters the chest wound killed him.

The Chief was not wearing a bulletproof vest. Gordon Mainhart, the only full-time officer left, would say years later that the Chief needed to send his new vest back. It was too small.

The elderly woman knitting saw someone limping not far from the Chief's cruiser. The person ducked down. Then the car drove off. Based on the blood at the scene, investigators believed the killer had been shot. Police were provided a description of a man with longish hair wearing aviator glasses. A composite sketch of that man was circulated in the media.

Only a teenaged boy heard the shots. Only the boy and his mother heard the Chief's call for help. Only an elderly woman saw the car and cruiser pull into the Agway lot.

Night falls quickly in December. So do the temperatures. It was below 20 degrees by sunset and dropping quickly. Pennsylvania State Police investigators had cordoned off the Agway parking lot and the area behind the two houses where Greg Adams struggled for his life.

Saxonburg Assistant Fire Chief Ben Cypher drove his RV over for use as a makeshift field command post. Volunteer firefighters stood by to secure the scene overnight. It was dark and cold, and the winding roads into town were icy. The State's crime scene unit in Greensburg wouldn't get there until the next morning.

In Saxonburg and the close-knit communities circling it, people were frightened, shocked and grieving. Many people locked their doors for the first time.

Mary Ann heard the car pull up to her house. It was past midnight and her eldest sister, Alida Yoezle, had driven five hours with their mother from Waldorf, Maryland, to Saxonburg. Alida was a "take charge" person, and minutes after getting that phone call saying Greg was killed she was already mentally ticking off what needed to be done.

She tossed some clothes into the suitcase, gave her husband a verbal list of what to do and what their two kids would need, and hopped into the car with her mother, who lived with the Yoezle family. Alida wasn't sure exactly what she would do once they reached Saxonburg but she knew she could handle it.

The two Adams' boys were sound asleep when they first arrived. Mary Ann came to the door in her pajamas. Her eyes were red. She was worn and in shock. As her sister and mother settled in after the long drive, Mary Ann heard her toddler son crying in his room.

She leaned over and whispered over the child, "It's okay. It's okay."

He looked at her. "Dad's here," he told her. "Dad's here."

Mary Ann could feel the tears welling yet again.

She knew in her heart Greg came by to say one last good-bye.

The police officers, more than 100 strong, walked through the icy rain from the Saxonburg Municipal building to the Fox Funeral home less than 200 feet away. They came from throughout the state, from departments large and small. Some were plain-clothed, most were in uniform. They filed into the funeral home with their badges shrouded in black, removed their hats, paused at the blue coffin of Chief Gregory Adams and moved on. The police "walk-through" to honor a fallen officer was a ritual to show unity, brotherhood and support for the family. This day it also reminded the officers, many from small departments like Saxonburg, no one is immune to the danger in law enforcement.

To Mary Ann Adams, the wake and sea of blue was a blur of grief. Others had made the funeral arrangements—picking the casket, ordering flowers, setting up the Catholic Church service. It was all surreal—going to the hospital the afternoon of December 4 to learn Greg was dead and now, days later, going to the wake and funeral where he lay in a casket.

The funeral director had tried to cover the cuts and bruises on her husband's face and head. But Mary Ann could still see the evidence of the beating, the struggle, the fight, beneath the mortician's makeup work.

She brought her eldest son, Ben, to the wake briefly. The boy, just shy of three, looked at the casket and his father. He saw the people gathered around. He didn't understand why. Years later, Robert Paroli, whose wife was the Chief's cousin, still remembered seeing the tiny boy next to the casket. He called it heartbreaking.

On the day of the funeral, the 150 police cars escorting the Chief's coffin to St. Joseph Roman Catholic Church in Cabot stretched for more than a half-mile. Members of the Saxonburg American Legion Post 683 and the Sarver Veterans of

Foreign Wars lined the church steps. As the church bell tolled, the veterans and officers snapped to attention as pallbearers carried the flag-draped casket into the church. At least 200 police officers crammed into the church with friends, family and officials. More than 400 waited outside.

The 18-member youth choir, with three folk guitarists strumming, sang softly during the service. There were songs like "Our Son Has Gone Away" and "Come to Me All You Who Labor and I Shall Give You Rest." The Rev. Howard Bich, the church pastor, tried to comfort the community and make sense of the killing.

"Gregory Adams said yes to his commitment as a policeman and said it with courage," the priest said. "He was obedient regarding his duty. He gave his life for his community. He won the good fight and he finished his race."

At the end of the funeral, the scent of incense rich in the church, people filed out behind the casket. The police officers followed the hearse to St. Mary's Cemetery in Herman where, after a three-volley final salute, the flag from his casket was neatly folded and presented to his widow.

In a burial plot within eyeshot of what would later become a police training facility, Gregory Adams was laid to rest.

In the hours after the funeral, Mary Ann went home with her children.

The priest returned to the rectory.

The people of Saxonburg returned to their lives, now keeping their doors secure.

Pennsylvania State Police investigators returned to the command center in the basement of the Saxonburg municipal building where the owner of the Saxonburg Hotel, Alfred "Fred" Gentile, brought pans filled with food to them as the worked.

Police throughout the state and New Jersey continued the search for a white Cougar and a man named Stanley J. Portas. And the sole full-time police officer left on the Saxonburg force, Gordon Mainhart, sent out a Teletype message via State Police Capt. Robert Palladino.

1. PATROLMAN GORDON MAINHART, SAXONBURG POLICE DEPARTMENT, AND SAXONBURG MAYOR, RELDON COOPER, WISH TO EXPRESS THEIR THANKS TO ALL THOSE WHO ATTENDED THE FUNERAL SERVICES OF CHIEF ADAMS.

2. THE UNDERSIGNED ALSO WISHES TO EXPRESS HIS GRATITUDE FOR THE DISPLAY OF SOLIDARITY EXPRESSED BY THE MORE THAN 350 MEMBERS OF OUR CHOSEN PROFESSION WHO GATHERED FOR THIS SAD OCCASION.

Chapter 2
The Search

Pennsylvania State Trooper Jim Poydence found himself staring at the New Jersey driver's license found in the snow at the murder scene, memorizing the information.

Stanley J. Portas, 50, of 41 S. Main Street, Phillipsburg, New Jersey.

Who was this man? Poydence wondered. What brought him to Saxonburg? Why would he shoot the Chief? Poydence hoped to find those answers as he and Trooper Albert Vish drove roughly five hours from the state police barracks in Butler to the address in New Jersey nearly 320 miles away listed on the license.

The day after the killing, he had called New Jersey officials to see what, if anything, they knew about the suspect. Phillipsburg Police Officer J. P. Stettner scouted the neighborhood and scoured the department's records. There was nothing the New Jersey officer could find on a Stanley Portas on South Main Street in town.

Now, on December 8, four days after the Chief was killed, Poydence and Vish were in New Jersey to check for themselves, ringing doorbells and knocking on doors along South Main Street in Phillipsburg, a town across the Delaware River from Easton, Pennsylvania, hoping at least one person could offer a shred of information about Portas.

What they discovered was initially disheartening: not a

single person had even heard of Stanley J. Portas.

On December 9, five days after the killing, Poydence and Vish were at the Phillipsburg Town Clerk's office. There they learned more discouraging news. There was no Stanley Portas registered to vote. There was no Stanley Portas paying taxes. There was no Stanley Portas listed as a resident. The troopers checked the local utility companies—no listing of a Stanley Portas getting a phone, electric or gas bill. Stanley Portas never applied for welfare.

They were luckier with the New Jersey Department of Motor Vehicles. They discovered Portas once had a driver's license in Richmond, Virginia, listing an address of 2325 West Broad Street, Richmond. While the two troopers kept digging through New Jersey motor vehicle records, another team of investigators went to Virginia. But it was in New Jersey where the investigators hoped to have the best luck unspooling information.

The troopers discovered Stanley Portas took the state driver's exam at the Phillipsburg Armory. When he took the exam, this man called Stanley Portas initially gave a Route 22 Bethlehem, Pennsylvania address—the address of the Holiday Inn across the river. Registry officials told Portas that the new license couldn't be sent to the Holiday Inn in another state. He needed a permanent, in-state address. Portas came back and gave the South Main Street address in New Jersey.

These investigative breadcrumbs left by Portas appeared to lead in a circle.

There was one last place for the Pennsylvania troopers to check: The Phillipsburg Post Office. If Portas lived in town, maybe someone there, maybe a mail carrier, would remember the name. It was a long shot but it was their only shot.

Poydence and Vish walked under the triple arched entrance into the post office building and approached the counter.

"Could you check to see if you have any information about a Stanley Portas receiving mail in town?" they asked.

The clerk ducked away for a few minutes and came back. "Sorry. Nothing."

The troopers turned to leave. Another dead end.

When the clerk called them back as he motioned to the rural mail carrier walking in. He asked the carrier if the name Stanley Portas sounded familiar.

The carrier paused. "Yeah, I remember forwarding mail for a Portas. Let me see if I can find that address," the carrier said, Poydence recalled.

The postal workers searched through forwarded mail stickers. There was one forwarding mail sticker left for 41 South Main Street.

The troopers wrote down the new address: RD #2, Phillipsburg.

Within 20 minutes, they were at the New Jersey State Police barracks in Washington, meeting with New Jersey State Police Sgt. Mike Gosden.

"Can you help us track whose address this is?" Poydence asked.

The sergeant made a few calls. He found the name of the woman who lived at the address and where she worked.

Sometimes you do find the needle in the haystack.

The New Jersey and Pennsylvania troopers drove directly to a local manufacturing plant and told the manager they needed to talk with one of the female workers. Now.

Could this be the start of the end of the search? As the troopers waited in the office for the woman to come in, they tried not to be too hopeful.

Jim Poydence showed her a driver's license photograph. "Do you know this man?"

"Never saw him before," she answered.

"Are you sure?" Poydence asked.

"I don't know him."

Jim Poydence pressed her again. "This guy's mail was forwarded to your house."

She was adamant. She told them she didn't know what they were talking about. She didn't know anyone named Portas, and she never received any mail for him.

Poydence tried again. "You sure? Why would his mail go to your house?"

She shook her head. She never saw him, didn't know him.

The troopers detected a bit of hesitancy and nervousness in the woman's voice. The troopers did their fair share of witness interviews over the years and paid close attention to the nuances of a voice, the shift of the body, the narrowing of the eyes, the clutching of arms. They could spot the "tells" in the language of the body even when the words said something else. As they talked with this woman, they knew there was more to learn.

What is she hiding? Why is she so reluctant to talk? Does she know where Stanley Portas is? Those questions pricked the troopers' minds as they walked out of the manufacturing plant on that cold December day.

Frustrated, Poydence and Vish drove back to the nearby orange-roofed Howard Johnson's Motor Lodge where they were staying. They were convinced this woman was stonewalling them. How could they get her to talk? How could they convince her to say where Portas was?

The next morning, the phone in the motel room rang.

Sgt. Gerald Logan, the New Jersey State Police Washington station commander, was on the line.

A woman called the barracks at 2 a.m. and wanted the desk officer to know she had lied to the troopers who came to talk to her, Logan told them. She knew who Stanley Portas was. She wanted to talk with them again.

Poydence hung up the phone and turned to Vish. Things were falling into place.

They met the woman again at her workplace around 10:15 in the morning on December 10.

There she told them the story of how she came to meet Portas.

She first met the guy in the photo along with his friend in the spring of 1980 at the Peke Inn in Phillipsburg, a landmark restaurant in town. The Peke Inn was a popular spot, with its four dining rooms, large mirrors and a cocktail lounge sporting a 60-seat wrap-around bar. People would go there to meet up, to drink, to host parties and weddings. She went there often enough to know the manager and other regulars. She saw the guy in the photo and his friend a few times that year at the Peke Inn. They had rounds and rounds of drinks. They laughed. They chatted. They told her they were from Georgia. They told someone else in the bar they were in the junk jewelry business in New York.

When the men were in town, they would usually come into the Peke Inn around noon or late evening. Once they claimed they were staying at the Holiday Inn nearby but when they invited her to their room it was at the Howard Johnson's.

The troopers discovered she was a very observant woman. She told them she once saw a receipt in the room for a Howard Johnson's in Atlanta. Portas had something on his upper left arm, a mark that was either a tattoo or a scar. Portas and his friend would pop into town at different times during the year. She was never sure when they would show up.

Then in the summer of 1980, the manager of the Peke Inn told her someone needed a favor. "Could you talk to Stanley over there?" So she strolled over to Stanley, who had a proposition for her.

He said he was living with his brother in town but now his brother was moving. He needed someplace to have mail sent. Could he use her address? He would pay her $50. Sure, she told him.

Two or three days later, mail addressed to Stanley Portas came to her house. She dutifully brought it over to the Peke Inn and handed the letter from the New Jersey Registry of Motor Vehicles to the manager. She wasn't sure where it went from there.

The last time she saw Portas, he promised to take her to New York with him when he came back to town. He told her he was first heading to California with his friend.

As they listened to the woman, Jim and his partner knew the suspect was long gone from the Howard Johnson's in town but maybe, just maybe, someone there remembered something else about the man.

Maybe, just maybe, the killer left something behind.

He did.

When Stanley Portas checked into Room 109 on February 1, 1980, then checked out on February 8, paying cash for the stay, he listed his workplace as P&M Distributors, 2325 W. Broad Street, Richmond, Virginia—a dummy business address and the same address on his Virginia driver's license.

At check-in, he listed the registration plate of a blue Chevrolet Impala he was driving. It was listed to Budget Rental in Allentown, Pennsylvania, a real company.

The troopers went to Allentown.

The owner of the car rental agency remembered Portas well. He was a very good customer. Portas had been renting cars for 30 weeks, on five separate occasions, starting in early 1980. He seemed like a good guy, always dressed nice. He wore plaid slacks and looked like a salesman. He was friendly but always seemed uptight. Once he came in with a partner, a bigger guy.

Portas rented the Impala for four weeks, from January 25, 1980, to February 22, 1980, and paid in cash. He always paid cash, the owner told them. That's what Portas preferred. He would hand over a credit card to hold the car but always left instructions not to put it through. Cash only. But the owner, Ken Smith, had made a copy of the credit card information and still had it.

"Oh, one more thing," the owner said. "There was that time we owed him money back on a deposit on his first rental."

The company wrote Portas a refund check. In 1980, canceled checks were returned in the mail to account holders to keep for their records. These original checks would show the date and which bank the check was cashed or deposited. It would also bear the signature of who cashed it on the back.

The manager flipped through the back files in his office as the troopers waited.

"Here it is," he told them, holding the $333.90 canceled check from Northeastern Bank of Pennsylvania, "the bank the rental company used."

It was deposited at the First National Bank in New Bedford, Massachusetts on July 29, 1980.

It was deposited into the account of a Lillian Webb of New Bedford, Massachusetts.

What was her tie to Stanley Portas, the troopers wondered? How does she play into this?

After the license bearing the name Stanley Portas was found at the murder scene, Pennsylvania State Police investigators issued a statewide alert to police departments. Check the motels in your area. Did anyone with that name ever check-in?

It didn't take long before information came in.

Police quickly learned Portas skipped from state to state, motel to motel. He appeared stateless and rootless. And he always seemed to be careful.

As Poydence and Vish had learned, Portas had turned in a Virginia license for a New Jersey license earlier in 1980—then applied for a duplicate license back in Virginia. Two licenses in two states. Portas had business cards printed for his company P&M Distributors in Richmond, Virginia. He claimed to be a jewelry distributor. The address he listed in Richmond, Virginia was a telephone answering service. His company was phony.

Pennsylvania State Police investigators, along with FBI agents in Pennsylvania, peeled back layer after layer of the man called Stanley Portas.

He appeared to be a ghost.

They kept searching.

In 1980, most business records were handwritten. Paperwork was kept in file cabinets. Sometimes key information police would need—such as a person's description—lived only in a person's memory. Digging out those snippets was time-consuming. Poydence and the others on the Pennsylvania State Police working the case knew they had to move fast to find Portas before the killer slipped away. Again.

Information was coming in quickly from the field.

Investigators learned Portas was stopped for drunken driving a year earlier in Henrico County in Virginia in January of 1979. Neither his photograph nor fingerprints were taken at the time—not unusual since the charge in Virginia then was a misdemeanor.

Portas stayed at the Fountain Inn on Route 22 in Altoona for about a week in November. The manager there said the guy appeared to be a salesman, came in late at night, paid cash for his room and told him some customers would be coming in the next day.

After that, Portas checked into the Friendship Inn in Greensburg on Route 30 on November 17, 1980, and left in December, the day after Chief Gregory Adams was killed. The maid named Flosie was walking by Portas' room around 11 in the morning of December 5 and saw the room window was open and the blinds were up. She could see cash atop the table inside. She went inside and found $110 and a note from Portas. The money, he wrote, was to pay the last four days of the room. The rest was a tip.

Jim and his colleagues later learned a Williamsport police lieutenant in 1979 foiled the robbery of Kinley jewelry store in Williamsport on a Sunday afternoon when he spotted a guy walking around with a walkie-talkie. Initially, the lieutenant thought the man was a state trooper working a case. Then the guy spotted the cruiser and ran. He was caught. So were a few others.

The suspects were part of a crew from Fall River, Massachusetts, a mill city not far from Providence, Rhode Island, that had been staking out the store for two weeks. That Sunday was supposed to be the big score, police learned. While the business was closed, one guy disabled the alarm system while another climbed up a ladder to the second floor, jimmied open a window and, using brand new Sears tools, cut a hole in the floor. Then he dropped into the jewelry store office. Police found a car a block away with radio equipment tuned to all of the local police department frequencies. The suspects, police later learned, had flown in from Providence to the airport in Avoca, Pennsylvania and rented cars.

The owner of the jewelry store remembered a man matching Portas' description in the business two weeks before the aborted heist.

The owner said the man told him he was looking for something nice for his wife. The owner brought out some pieces. The man asked if there was anything nicer, the owner told police, so he went into the back of the store and brought out pricier jewelry.

The spot where the owner went, where the "good stuff" was kept, was the area targeted by the thieves. Could that "customer" have been Portas? Could Portas have been staking out yet another jewelry store at the time of the killing, this one a family-run business not far from where Greg Adams was killed? Or was Portas looking at some other, larger stores and just got lost?

But it was that Greensburg motel stay in November of 1980, shortly before the killing, which intrigued Poydence and his colleagues the most. That was when Portas crossed paths with a state trooper on November 18, 1980.

Portas, who claimed to be a "junk jewelry salesman," had started his car in the motel parking lot and left it running — but accidentally locked the keys inside. He took a towel from his motel room, shoved it into the car exhaust pipe to stall it out then called State Police for assistance.

A helpful trooper arrived, drove Portas to a dealership owned by a well-known businessman, Bud Smail, to get a new key. Portas handed over a ten-dollar bill for the $3.50 key and told the clerk to keep the change. The trooper then brought Portas back to the vehicle. The trooper took Portas' license information and made an incident report.

The next day, Portas swung by the State Police barracks and asked for the trooper who helped him. When the desk officer told him the trooper wasn't there, Portas set a brown bag on the counter.

"A small token of my appreciation," he told the desk officer, investigators later recalled. "Can you get this to him?" It was a fifth of whiskey.

Then the man who called himself Stanley Portas drove off in his rented car.

With that brand new key in the ignition.

That duplicate key was made after the Pennsylvania dealership called a business in Massachusetts where Portas had rented the Mercury Cougar to get the key number.

That place was Shea Rose Lincoln Mercury in Taunton, Massachusetts.

Another tie to Massachusetts.

This could be the key to where Stanley Portas might be.

The Federal Bureau of Investigation agents working in the New Castle "resident agency" office in Pennsylvania had been working on the murder investigation from the start. When the first call went out Dec. 4, 1980, that the Saxonburg Police Chief was shot and killed, Agent Peter McCann and another agent, G. Victor Reuschlein, bolted out to Saxonburg. There were four small "resident agency" offices like the one in New Castle in Pennsylvania at the time, with the main FBI office in Pittsburgh. The agents in these "resident agency" offices handled cases in specific, geographic areas and always made it a point to cooperate with Pennsylvania State Police.

This case had the FBI's full attention.

Two things needed to be checked out immediately in the days after the killing. A check written to Stanley J. Portas had been cashed at the First National Bank in Massachusetts. The car Portas was driving was traced to a rental business in Taunton.

McCann called his counterpart and friend in the New Bedford, Massachusetts, FBI office for help.

FBI Special Agent George Bates had been working in the four-man New Bedford office for nearly ten years. Before that, he had worked in Springfield, Illinois, with McCann, a man he considered one of his best friends. Bates prided himself on his ability to work closely with the Massachusetts State Police. His office in the federal Hastings Building was two blocks away from the District Attorney's downtown office and he would, whenever needed, stroll over to talk with the troopers assigned to the investigative unit there.

The call to Bates from the Pennsylvania FBI office was

simple: "The guy who killed a police chief might be in your area. His name is Stanley Portas. It appears he rented a car from a Taunton business. Can you check it out?"

Bates drove 20 minutes north to pay the place a visit.

At first the manager in the rental office suffered amnesia with a touch of attitude.

Then, Bates would later recall, he not so politely reminded him this was a homicide—and a federal case since the killer crossed state lines to avoid prosecution. Did he really want to stonewall the FBI? Did he really want to open himself up to possible prosecution? Did he really want to do that?

The manager's memory quickly returned. Stanley Portas was staying at a motel on Route 44 the next town over in Raynham, Massachusetts, he told the agent. Bates left the car rental business as fast as he could and drove there.

The Town and Country Motel on Route 44 across from a bowling alley and pub was nondescript, one of those pullovers so common in the 50s and 60s. There was an outdoor pool in the front and rooms to the side. It was clean and quiet. Rarely were police called there. Bates first spoke to the manager, then a chambermaid.

"Do you remember anything about this guy?" he asked the maid.

"Oh, yes. I can describe him," she answered, Bates recalled.

Could this be it? Could they be close to catching this cop killer? Bates knew someone who worked at the electric company in New Bedford who was also a good sketch artist. Maybe they could get a good sketch of the suspect.

"Do you think you could describe the guy to an artist?" Bates asked the woman.

"No problem," she told him.

It didn't take long to make the arrangements to bring the woman to the New Bedford FBI office where she described the man known as Stanley Portas to the artist.

Bates looked at the pencil sketch once it was done.

This is the killer.

This is who we are after.

One of the first persons he showed the sketch to was Massachusetts State Police Detective Lt. Gordon Clarkson at the Bristol County District Attorney's Office in New Bedford.

Clarkson was a former New Bedford police captain who made a lateral transfer onto the State Police and was now in charge of the special state police unit—called Crime Prevention and Control, CPAC for short—at the prosecutor's office.

In Massachusetts, a plain-clothed state police unit is assigned to each county prosecutor's office to handle everything from murders to white collar crimes to larger drug investigations. Bates felt comfortable showing Clarkson the sketch. If this sketch depicted someone local, the troopers in his office would recognize him.

"You know who that is," Clarkson told him, looking at the sketch, Bates recalled.

"No, I don't know who it is or I wouldn't be asking you," Bates answered.

"That's Donald Webb."

Bates later learned Stanley Portas died on February 28, 1956, at age 25 of rheumatic heart disease, leaving behind a young pregnant wife. He was buried in St. John's Cemetery in New Bedford, Massachusetts.

Donald Eugene Webb, the man depicted in the sketch, lived in New Bedford and was married to Portas' widow. He often used Stanley Portas as one of his many aliases.

Webb was a member of the so-called Fall River Gang, a loose group of thieves who roamed the East Coast, burglarizing jewelry stores as well as homes and businesses with lots of cash. At the time of the Chief's killing, he was wanted in Colonie, New York, where he skipped out on a court date in an attempted burglary. He also operated a string of gaming and poker machines, all illegal in Massachusetts at that time. Webb was the type of guy who liked the ladies, liked to tip big and was always looking for the next job. He was a tough guy who hinted at Providence mob ties.

He married Portas' widow, Lillian, on February 28, 1961, on the sixth anniversary of Portas' death—and helped raise her son, who was named Stanley after his biological father.

Stanley, who took Webb's surname even though he was never officially adopted, was working as a New Bedford cop in 1980.

Lillian worked a wide range of jobs in the city early on, sometimes as a hostess, sometimes as a singer before landing in the office at a local company. She was a very attractive woman, always put together nicely, a woman men of all ages noticed.

At one point, Donald and Lillian ran a small sandwich shop in New Bedford's South End on Rodney French Boulevard next to the Washington Club and a young newspaper carrier, Paul Boudreau, who would later become a New Bedford cop, would stop in once a week. He would order the same thing each time: two burgers and a piece of squash pie. And he would stare at the woman who looked like a movie star to him.

Lillian sometimes sang in clubs, including the Orchid Club in the South End of the city, people in the city recalled. That earned her the nickname "Dakota Lil," an apparent reference to the actress Marie Windsor who played the title character in the 1950 Western film about a Secret Service agent who enlists the help of a singer/forger to help catch the Hole-in-the-Wall Gang.

Bates, the FBI agent, was getting a quick lesson from the State Police lieutenant about who Donald Eugene Webb was and with whom he associated.

What Bates didn't know as he shared information about the suspected cop killer was the lieutenant was very friendly with Webb's wife.

By the time he did, it was too late.

The world, Bates would later say, is not as big as everyone believes.

In the days after the killing, Pennsylvania State Police released a formal statement letting the public know investigators wanted to speak with a man named Donald Eugene Webb about the case. Webb was using the alias of Stanley Portas, the name on the license found at the murder scene, State Police Lt. Francis Walton told reporters. He stopped short of calling Webb a suspect. The news made newspaper headlines across Pennsylvania and was top news on television and radio stations. Residents were buoyed by hope the killer, once identified, would be caught soon.

If Donald Webb was quickly becoming a familiar name in the Greater Saxonburg, Pennsylvania area, the same wasn't true in Massachusetts where he had been living. The local daily newspapers in the cities he frequented—New Bedford, Fall River and Taunton—had no mention in those early weeks about the search for Webb. The focus was on the Christmas season, the 52 hostages held in Iran since November 4, 1979, at the American Embassy, school committee meetings, and fuel costs.

There was a front-page story in the *Herald-News* of Fall River about a Milford, Massachusetts, police sergeant named Walter Conley, in a community an hour away, who was shot to death as he carried $50 worth of pennies from one bank to another. There were later stories about the New Year's baby, the record cold temperatures, incoming President Ronald Reagan, depleted snow plowing budgets and town water projects. There were ads on the broadsheet pages, in this time when local newspapers were thick, for bib farmer jeans for $18.98 at the local Kmart and pork chops for $1.38 at the Food Mart.

There were news stories about organized crime, of course. The reputed head of the Providence mob, Raymond L.S. Patriarca, 72, had been arrested December 4, 1980, the same day Chief Adams was killed, accused of ordering the 1965 hit on Raymond "Baby" Curcio, a drug addict who made the mistake of breaking into his older brother's house.

Another man, Gerard T. "The Frenchman" Ouimette originally from Fall River, was charged in early 1981 (and later acquitted) in the 1965 killing of an East Greenwich businessman whose body was found in Rehoboth, Massachusetts with a bullet to the head. There was a Brinks truck robbery in Boston, where three masked men disarmed a guard and made off with $153,500. It was clear to newspaper readers that police investigating organized crime in the region were busy in late 1980 and early 1981.

But if law enforcement knew a cop killer with ties, however tenuous, to the mob could be in the area, that fact was well under the general public's radar in Massachusetts. There was no one in the public to recognize him and call authorities because, outside that circle of investigators and the suspect's family and friends, few knew he was wanted. If he were in the New Bedford area, drinking at a Veterans of Foreign Wars post or one of the many darkened bars in the city, no one would think it necessary to drop a dime into the pay phone on the wall.

Even though the average person in Massachusetts may have been ignorant about the case, the police investigation still seemed to be moving quickly. It appeared, though, Donald Webb was moving faster and no one who knew the accused killer was cooperating with authorities. The FBI tried to interview the suspect's wife on December 17, 1980, about the car rental refund check she cashed. "Go talk to my attorney," they were told.

A few days later, on December 22, they interviewed Genita Martins, the girlfriend of David Hutchins. Hutchins was a member of the Fall River Gang and considered a master in disabling alarms—the "go to" person for most of the heists.

The investigators learned from her that earlier in the year, before the killing, Webb had stayed in motels in Brockton and Raynham, Massachusetts. In this era before cell phones, he even had his own hardline installed at Genita Martin's apartment in Taunton to get calls.

The last time she said she saw Webb was in November 1980, a month before the killing of the Chief, in the parking lot of the Town and Country Motel in Raynham. She told them he was driving a white Mercury Cougar and was registered at the motel under the name Stanley Portas.

If she wanted to reach Webb for any reason, Genita said she would call his wife on a Sunday and leave a message. He would call back from a pay phone. The last time she called was two days earlier, on December 20, she told investigators.

Genita informed investigators that Lillian told her Webb had called. He was in trouble and would be laying low.

"Tear up my number," Genita recalled Lillian telling her. "Tear it up and don't call back."

The FBI and the Pennsylvania State Police had the house under surveillance.

Investigators knew more about where Donald Eugene Webb had been before Saxonburg Police Chief Greg Adams was killed. What they didn't know was where he was now.

FBI agent George Bates and Massachusetts State Police Corporal Paul Fitzgerald peered out the first floor window overlooking the small apartment complex parking lot on Hart Street in Taunton, Massachusetts, not far from Route 140, the highway into New Bedford, and Route 24, the main highway to Boston from the area. They got a tip earlier that day that Webb would be stopping by one of the apartments and the manager let them use an empty apartment for surveillance. Neither of the men brought any food. Or chairs. They didn't expect to be there very long.

The view from the apartment was perfect. They could see every car driving in. They could see every person getting out of those cars. When Webb drove in, it would be over. Done.

The tough part was this waiting. It was boring. Corporal Fitzgerald knew they couldn't keep their eyes off the driveway and lot. They couldn't leave the spot. He remembered another time when he and fellow trooper Patrick Hunt were on a stakeout with a cop from a local department trying to catch a bank robber.

The other cop got up at noon and left for an hour. It was lunchtime, he told the incredulous troopers, and he always broke for lunch. That wasn't the way Fitzgerald and Bates worked as they stood in the window, waiting and watching this December 1980 morning in Taunton, less than a week after getting word the cop killer was likely in Massachusetts. There was no leaving the apartment until they saw Webb.

They stayed at the window throughout the day. As night fell, they could see the headlights of each vehicle pull into the driveway and the taillights as each parked. They could see, under the parking lot lights, the drivers and passengers. They scanned the faces through binoculars. The two stood guard at the window, watching throughout the night until daybreak. It was just one of several long days a rotating group of investigators would spend watching that apartment and the parking lot below.

Webb never showed up. The main focus, though, was still on the city 24 miles and a half-hour drive south of Taunton: New Bedford. That was where Webb's wife was. That was where his life was.

Investigators from three agencies and four states had converged in the waterfront city where they believed someone was helping hide the killer. Based on the two different blood types found at the murder scene, they were convinced Webb had been shot and wounded but no hospitals in the region reported a man matching his description seeking treatment for a gunshot wound. The person treating him was discreet and as secretive as the killer. It had to be someone Webb knew.

Pennsylvania State Trooper John Crede flew up to Massachusetts with a few other troopers in mid-December after spending three days in Richmond, Virginia. He had been in Virginia with Pennsylvania Trooper Frank Groelmunt, gathering more details about the suspected killer's associates and tracking where the Fall River gang had been before the deadly encounter in Saxonburg.

The gang's "business" calls in Virginia went to a telephone answering service in a run-down building. The troopers discovered in Virginia that Webb and his cohorts stayed at what seemed to be their favorite motel chain, Howard Johnson's. The men were polite to the staff, were sticklers for cleanliness, and always kept their shoes shined. They dressed well, tipped even better and stayed off the radar of the Henrico Sheriff's Department.

Now, Pennsylvania troopers were concentrating on Massachusetts where they learned Webb had rented a car and his wife cashed a rental car refund check for another vehicle. The Pennsylvania troopers were staying in a waterfront motel in Fairhaven, Massachusetts, called *The Skipper*, across the bridge from New Bedford, owned by Ed Dinis.

Dinis was best known outside the area as the man who, when he was District Attorney, prosecuted Sen. Edward Kennedy in the drowning death of a young woman in Chappaquiddick. The troopers expected to stay in the motel until Webb, officially wanted in New York State as a fugitive, was caught. They planned a short stay.

The Pennsylvania investigators paired with Massachusetts state police officers assigned to the District Attorney's Office who would help them maneuver the area—both geographically and politically. The arrangement appeared to be working well.

The hunt for Greg Adams' killer was personal for John Crede. The two grew up on the same street when they lived in Natrona Heights. When Crede's family later moved, they gave the Adams' their St. Bernard dog. He fondly remembered those carefree childhood times and he never forgot his friend. John Crede lost touch with Greg Adams in those pre-social media days but later their adult lives—and law enforcement careers—would sometimes cross. As a state trooper in the Butler barracks, Crede's area covered Saxonburg, the small town Adams was working as the Police Chief.

Now, Crede was nearly 600 miles away from Saxonburg, working with a Massachusetts state police sergeant named Bruce Gordon, trying to find Adams' killer. The two spent hours staking out houses and businesses and bars and restaurants and anyone Webb might seek out. They weren't sure who might help or where Webb might turn up. Crede and the others from Pennsylvania weren't prepared for the interwoven relationships in the city.

When they made a surprise visit to a small New Bedford South End restaurant to talk with Webb's wife who was working there as a hostess, John Crede was stunned to see her sitting with Clarkson, the guy in charge of the Massachusetts State

Police investigative unit. Wasn't Clarkson just in the District Attorney's Office a day or two earlier when they were talking about the case? Talking about what Lillian Webb might know and if she was hiding him?

He didn't know what to make of this. Was Clarkson tipping the wife off or was he trying to get her to talk? Unease hung over the Pennsylvania investigators as they weaved through the personal dynamics and relationships in the city. Were people here helping or hiding?

While Webb's wife and friends steadfastly refused to cooperate with authorities, the investigators continued to follow those close to the killer. Houses, apartments and businesses were staked out. Criminal associates as well as Webb's wife were followed. The frustrating work was 24/7 but New Bedford was a small city where, Crede hoped, secrets didn't stay hidden for long. Crede held fast to the hope he could arrest Webb and bring him back to Pennsylvania before Christmas. He knew the holiday would be difficult for Greg Adams' grieving family.

An arrest would be a Christmas gift of justice to everyone.

It was just before eight in the morning—7:50 a.m. is what Warwick, Rhode Island, Officer Charles Carr, who was wrapping up his overnight shift, would later report—on December 21, 1980, when a 1980 white Mercury Cougar XR7 bearing Massachusetts license plate 783 CHE was found in the parking lot of the Howard Johnson's motel on Jefferson Boulevard in Warwick, Rhode Island. The plates matched the car on the BOLO (Be On the Look Out) alert issued in connection with the slaying of Saxonburg Police Chief Greg Adams.

Pennsylvania, Rhode Island, and Massachusetts state troopers drove to the scene. So did FBI agents. This was a big break in the case, Crede thought as he stood near the car as temperatures hovered between 10 and 17 degrees. This meant the suspect was in the area. This meant they could be close. Crede was already trying to figure out how quickly Pennsylvania crime scene technicians could get there, how quickly the car could be brought back as evidence.

"We want to process the car," Crede told the Warwick police department supervisor who arrived at the scene.

Crede and Massachusetts State Police Sgt. Dan Lowney were dumbfounded by the chilly answer.

"No. The car is in our city; it is in our jurisdiction," they both recalled being told.

Lowney could see the Pennsylvania trooper tense up. This was an emotional case for Crede and the other Pennsylvania troopers who were tracking Webb in New England. This was a police chief they knew, someone they worked with. This was personal. They didn't want to leave the examination of the car, this key piece of evidence, in the hands of people they didn't know who worked in a department they had no dealings with. They didn't want any mistakes.

Crede's answer was sharp. "We will handle it."

The Warwick cop didn't back down, investigators recalled. "No, we will do it."

The men's voices quickly rose.

Within minutes, Crede was threatened with arrest. Both he and Lowney recalled handcuffs were brought out.

Rhode Island State Police Lt. Joe Green stepped in.

"Back down," he said firmly, Crede would later remember.

The FBI agent in charge of the Providence office, Joe Smith, looked around the group. He knew he needed to diffuse the situation. "The FBI is taking over the scene," he told them. "We will handle it."

The car was towed and Rhode Island State Police obtained a search warrant for the vehicle. The evidence collected was first turned over to the FBI for examination, then to the Pennsylvania State Police. There were cigarette butts found in the rear ashtray. Webb, police were told, didn't smoke. They now wondered: Who else was in the car?

FBI crime scene experts also later found the Mercury Cougar interior had been cleaned. But not enough. There is always blood left behind, forensic experts will tell you. It was no different in this case. Blood soaked into the driver's side floor and carpet. One stain was the size of a baseball. It was Type O. It was the same blood type as Donald Eugene Webb, the man who rented the car using the alias Stanley J. Portas.

As Christmas neared, investigators working in Massachusetts appeared to be no closer to finding Webb.

"Take a break," Crede's boss told the Pennsylvania troopers there. "I'm bringing you guys home for Christmas." So, at 8 in the morning on December 24, 1980, the four Pennsylvania troopers hopped on a plane from Providence. A snowstorm hit. Pittsburgh was snowed in and the plane was rerouted to Columbus, Ohio. They finally got home on Christmas at 3:00 in the morning. The day after Christmas, they were back on a plane and back in New Bedford.

On Christmas Eve, as the other troopers struggled to get home from Massachusetts, Jim Poydence was in his second floor office at the Butler State Police barracks, typing out the needed paperwork on his Underwood to get an arrest warrant for Donald Eugene Webb, aka Donald Eugene Perkins, Stanley J. Portas and S. John Portas, on a charge of murder.

He noted in the three-page complaint and supporting affidavit, number B789765-4, to be submitted to District Judge James H. Galbreath, the details of what investigators painstakingly uncovered since the December 4 murder.

Chief Gregory Adams was beaten and shot in his left side and chest with a .25 caliber Colt pistol. The Chief was dead on arrival at Butler County Memorial Hospital at approximately 3:25 p.m. There were two different types of blood found at the scene: that of the Chief and the killer.

The New Jersey driver's license bearing the name Stanley J. Portas of 41 South Main Street, Phillipsburg, New Jersey, was found several feet from where the suspect's car was. Someone saw the Chief standing and talking to a man in a white car.

Stanley J. Portas died in 1956 and was buried in Dartmouth, Massachusetts.

His widow was married to Donald Webb. The 1980 white Mercury Cougar was rented under the name Stanley Portas. That car was found December 21 at approximately 7:50 a.m. in a motel parking lot in Warwick, Rhode Island. Blood in that car was Type O, the same blood type as Donald E. Webb.

The affidavit was clear and concise. It did not list the difficulty — and luck — that went into uncovering some of the information. It did not note that, at any time, the trail could have gone dead. What if the mailman hadn't walked in that day to give the troopers a new address for "Stanley Portas?" What if "Stanley" hadn't called Pennsylvania police for help with his car? What if the canceled check at the car rental business had been thrown away? None of that was lost on Poydence as he typed up the court paperwork, asking the judge to charge Donald Eugene Webb, DOB 7-14-28, with first-degree murder.

The warrant was issued by Judge Galbreath minutes after Poydence handed it to the court in Saxonburg.

A group of Rhode Island mobsters were hosting a big New Year's Eve party at the Dunfey's Hyannis Resort on Cape Cod, police were told. Some members of the Fall River Gang were expected to be there: Frank Lach, David Hutchins and, of course, Donald Webb.

FBI Special Agent George Bates, along with Pennsylvania State Police and Massachusetts State Police, drove out to Hyannis to meet with police officers on the Cape to craft a plan to catch Webb.

"This is what we suspect," Bates told the group. "Donald Webb will be coming out here for a New Years Eve party. He will likely be in a car driven by one of his buddies. We will give you the make and model of the car. If you see the car, don't stop it. Don't do anything. We will be waiting."

Close to 20 members of law enforcement were at the hotel. Some of the Federal agents and State Police huddled in rooms throughout the hotel. All of the entrances and exits were covered. From their vantage, some could see the cars pulling up to the building and who got out.

Inside the hotel, the investigators were listening to the police radio. The car was coming up the street. It was the one they were told Webb would be in. Were there two people in the front seat? Could one be Webb?

"Hold on. This may be it," someone radioed.

Someone saw the Barnstable police cruiser. It was behind the car.

The driver made a quick turn into a parking lot and behind a building, briefly disappearing. Then it made a quick right. The town cruiser kept following it.

When the car was finally stopped, there was just one person inside.

An informant later told police Webb had rolled out of the car into a weed-strewn lot in the brief seconds the vehicle was out of sight.

If it was true, Donald Eugene Webb escaped the carefully drawn net once again.

Chapter 3
Two Lives Collide

Pennsylvania troopers and FBI agents tugged at the information threads in police reports, prison records and military records to unravel the aliases and complicated weave of Donald Eugene Webb's life. He was a phantom. His name changed with each move, seemingly with each arrest.

He was born Donald Perkins in Oklahoma City, Oklahoma on July 14, 1928, the younger of two sons to Dorice and Sunshine Perkins. When his mother died of tuberculosis in 1930 when he was two, his father abandoned the boys at the funeral, Massachusetts prison records note. Eventually, both boys went to live with their grandfather and his wife in Kansas City, Missouri. Webb, according to a 1976 Massachusetts prison diagnostic summary and parole reports, described his grandfather as "a peach" and his wife as "wicked." The grandmother was overbearing and "at times an overzealous physical disciplinarian." The two brothers ran away a couple of times. The first time was when Webb was ten.

One of his earliest memories was a doctor bringing him to a medical convention as an "exhibit." Why remains unclear in the Massachusetts prison file, but it may have been tied to his diagnosis with Osler-Weber Syndrome, a rare and incurable genetic blood disorder that often leads to excessive bleeding. (Investigators would later check with Veteran Administration hospitals and doctors after the Chief's killing to see if anyone matching Webb's description sought treatment for the disorder. No one did.)

Webb and his brother, four years older, appeared to be polar opposites. His brother, William, was studious and, as an adult, eventually moved to California to work in the entertainment industry in the 1970s in what was described to police as a successful career. Donald, who unofficially took his grandparents' last name of Webb, hated school and ran with a very different crowd, often getting into trouble.

The grandparents apparently tried to rein in the younger and often rebellious Donald. They sent him to parochial schools—first St. James Grammar School in Kansas City then St. James High School, where he was labeled "mischievous" and rebelled against the schools' rigidity and discipline.

Midway through his sophomore year, at age 16, he ran away again and ended up in Colorado where he found work on a farm. For two years, he stayed away, working seasonal and part-time jobs, traveling through the Southwest and California where he was arrested at least twice in California for petty theft and drunkenness, winding up briefly in a detention home before heading back to Kansas City and his grandfather's home.

He enlisted in the U.S. Air Force at age 20 under his birth name, Donald Perkins, and wound up at one point at Otis Air Force base in Massachusetts, where he later told Boston police he helped guard the cash payrolls. He didn't last long. He later admitted to prison officials he "couldn't adjust" to the discipline needed in the military, clashed with superior officers and, after a 1950 drunken driving arrest in Middleboro, he was booted out of the service in 1951, getting a "dishonorable discharge."

He wound up in Taunton, Massachusetts, at first, working at a machine shop, and was living in a downtown hotel when he and another man early on September 10, 1951, stole a safe from a barracks at the Otis Air Force base on Cape Cod (now called Otis Air National Guard base).

The pair drove with the safe to Taunton, opening it off Briggs Street. They split the $30 inside. Taunton Police Captain John McGaughran and State Trooper George Hacking later recovered the safe in the Taunton River near what was then a new sewage plant. Donald Perkins later pleaded guilty and was sentenced to a year in jail.

From there, he went to Providence, Rhode Island, where he worked what were described as menial jobs he couldn't keep for long. In 1953, he was convicted of breaking and entering and larceny in Rhode Island and given a three-year suspended sentence.

In the 1950s, he worked a series of jobs in Providence, Rhode Island, including at Bum's Pullman diner, Acme Casting Co. and the Tally-Ho Restaurant. By 1955, he claimed he needed to pay off gambling debts so he figured out a way to get quick cash. He would steal it. He first swiped an Oldsmobile sedan from a Sears parking lot June 29 after smashing the vent window. The next day, with a buddy from Brockton, Massachusetts named Stephen Roukous (who would later be charged in a 1968 Brink's armored truck heist in Boston) as the getaway driver, he strode into the Grove Hall Savings Bank in Roxbury on Blue Hill Avenue carrying a handgun and a green pillowcase.

He first demanded cash from a terrified teller who stepped back and accidentally set off the silent alarm. Donald then jumped over the counter, waving the gun and stuffing $5,145 in the pillowcase and his pockets. He ran back to the waiting car and his buddy drove off—only to get stuck in traffic. Donald jumped out of the car and ran into an alley, where he tried to hide behind some ash barrels.

Two officers gave chase, one spotting the crouching Donald, and fired a shot, creasing the suspect's head. Donald then stuck a gun in another patrolman's stomach during a scuffle, threatening to kill him, but the officer was able to kick the weapon from his hand. Donald was charged with larceny, bank robbery and conspiracy to commit murder. He was 26 years old.

He told police at the time he was working as a bookie. "I started gambling with my take from the numbers and horses and lost," he was quoted by police in the *Boston Globe* as saying at the time. "I couldn't pay up to the mob and I was supposed to pay once a week."

"All the Providence banks and loan offices had already been robbed, so I decided to come to Boston," he told police. He said he owed about $1,500. "I don't know whether they'd kill me or not, but they would have made things awfully rough. I don't think they'd kill anyone for that kind of money," he was quoted as saying.

Webb, who insisted his buddy had nothing to do with the robbery, was acquitted of the conspiracy to commit murder charge but convicted of larceny and bank robbery and sentenced to 12 to 15 years. However, he was paroled after five years, moved to New Bedford and worked as a night manager at a restaurant.

In 1962, under the name Donald Perkins, he married the widowed Lillian Correia Portas on February 28 at the Town Hall in Dartmouth, Massachusetts.

They married on the sixth anniversary of her first husband's death.

Lillian Carmo Correia was nineteen when she married her first husband, Stanley J. Portas, in 1953. He listed his occupation as a cloth cutter; she was a kick presser. They married at Our Lady of Mt. Carmel Church in New Bedford, followed by a reception at Monte Pio Hall.

The bride carried a prayer book with a white orchid and wore a gown of imported Chantilly lace over ivory satin with long tapered sleeves. The groom's mother wore a black dress; the bride's mother wore blue with black accessories. Three years later, while Lillian was pregnant with the couple's first child, Stanley died at age 25 of what was listed on his death certificate as rheumatic heart disease.

Lillian's son, Stanley, born seven months after his father's death, was six when she married Donald. (By December 1980, when Chief Adams was killed, Stanley was a New Bedford cop, appointed to the law enforcement job in May 1980 after working for five years as a police cadet on the city's force. He was using the last name of Webb.)

Donald listed his occupation as a restaurant owner. She was a singer and hostess who, one prison report noted, was "faithful 'through thick and thin.' ... It appears to be a very one-sided relationship to which he contributed little constructive effort."

Donald described his wife, according to the prison report, as a "strong, dominating, aggressive woman," and the few friends he had were "generally rather undesirable types."

In February of 1965, Donald Perkins finally changed his name legally to Donald Webb. He noted in the petition to the Massachusetts court that he was known by the last name of Webb until he entered the U.S. Air Force. He said Webb was the name he used in business and socially.

While his wife was described as a "significant positive influence," the marriage did little to keep Webb straight. In 1968, he was convicted of passing counterfeit money in 1966 in Taunton, Massachusetts and sentenced to 26 months at the Louisburg Federal Prison. He was paroled in July of 1970 and got a job at New England Plating Company in New Bedford, Massachusetts. A few months later, in October of 1970, he was charged with breaking and entering into a home in Warren, Massachusetts.

It was clear by this time Webb was a criminal on the move in the Northeast, undeterred by the threat of prison.

On April 14, 1972, shortly before 12:30 in the afternoon, he was caught by police bolting out of a Waterbury, Connecticut, house after stealing $477.67. When the two officers searched him, they found burglary tools and a .25 Colt automatic, fully loaded with one shell in the chamber. His attorney told him he would likely be sent back to federal prison for violating parole. Instead, Webb was released on $5,000 bond, jumped bail and was back on the run—until he was arrested yet again, this time in Albany, New York, on charges of possession of a blackjack and possession of burglary tools.

By the time the Waterbury case went to court three years later, Webb was already serving a five-year sentence at the New York State Prison in Dannemora, New York, on the Albany charges.

Webb wound up serving his Connecticut sentence at the

state prison in Massachusetts, MCI Walpole later renamed Cedar Junction State Prison, through an interstate compact. There, his wife and stepson would regularly visit him.

Based on Webb's criminal record, the Pennsylvania and FBI investigators knew they were dealing with a career criminal.

They knew they also needed to know the story behind the charges to learn more about the man: whom he knew, what he liked, where he might hide.

They tracked down his brother in California and learned the two hadn't talked in years. They discovered Webb's father moved to New Orleans where he ran a club and had been married three times. They were told Webb had the name "Ann" tattooed on his chest and Don between his right thumb and index finger. They never figured out who Ann was. Later, a few agents wondered if those tattoos even existed or if they were mentioned to confuse investigators. He dressed sharp for 1980 —plaid pants and polyester shirts—and was a big tipper. That was what waitresses noticed—those big tips. And he answered to many names.

Webb wasn't dumb. His IQ reportedly was 108, considered average as were his grades in school, and he ran with a crew of breaking and entering cons who roamed the East Coast for jobs. The crew, based in Fall River, Massachusetts, was known for slick heists. Webb was the scout. Another guy, David Hutchins, was the alarm guy. Frank Lach, heavyset and balding, was the break-in guy. There were a few others who came and went. It was a changing group, coming together for a score then disbanding. Often they were caught. Occasionally they weren't.

The marks they picked ranged from Chinese restaurant owners known to keep thousands in cash in safes at home to homeowners with some high-priced items in drawers or on the walls, to the jewelry stores, small and large, along the East Coast.

Sometimes they scanned the obituaries in newspapers and targeted the homes of the mourners who were at wakes or funerals. They took cash and anything that could easily be turned into cash. Local detectives, even after retiring, would describe the group's heists with professional awe. The jobs were generally clean, done with precision and criminal art: the disabled alarms, the creative methods used to break into businesses, the scams to map out the marks. The detectives who tracked the Fall River Gang, as it was commonly called, could see these guys were pros and took their "jobs" seriously—even though they were often arrested.

In the late 1970s and in 1980, Webb sometimes posed as a jewelry salesman and stopped into shops along the mid-Atlantic area. At one store he posed as a high-rolling customer looking for high-end jewelry for his wife.

In Virginia, he set up a phony business, complete with business cards, for his "jewelry sales." The Gang often preyed on businesses and people in towns or cities far from their home base. They usually didn't rob where they slept.

Webb was a con man and good at it. He was a smooth talker who could spin convincing stories. He posed as a jewelry salesman to talk up the managers and owners of jewelry stores or posed as a customer to figure out where the "good stuff" was kept. He could sweet talk waitresses and women he met in bars to do favors or provide information. He was slick and he was shrewd.

But Webb and his crew weren't slick enough for an upstate New York couple, Genevieve and Francis Truax, both in their 70s.

It was around 11 in the morning on January 5, 1979, in Colonie, New York, a city just outside Albany, when two men rang the back doorbell at the Truax's Central Avenue home. Mrs. Truax opened the door and saw two men on the back porch.

The men said they were putting in sewers and needed to inspect her cellar.

She looked the men up and down.

They asked if her husband was home.

"Yes," she answered and called her husband to the door. "Can I see some identification?" she then demanded from the men.

One flashed a silver badge tucked inside a beat-up wallet. She could see just one word on it: "Private."

She asked who they worked for.

"The City," one man said.

"The State," said the other.

The men said they were water inspectors and wanted to see what the cellar looked like, just in case there were any problems down the line.

As her husband stayed on the stairs, she took the men to the cellar and waited with them.

They asked about the water heater, the size and who installed it. They asked about the sump pump. One of the men was writing on a stack of papers as they walked through the basement.

As the two men talked, she saw a pair of men's legs pass by the cellar window. The man was heading to the back door.

The two men followed her eyes.

"Don't worry. He's with us, one told her. Can your husband come down to the basement, too?"

Her husband stayed by the stairs.

After a few minutes, the two men went back upstairs and left.

Mrs. Truax watched them hop in a red car, then saw a third person get in the back.

It didn't sit right with her. She jotted down the license plate number, 931ZAD, then called the police.

The car took off eastbound in a bit of a hurry, she later told police.

Around 5:45 that evening, Officer Marvin Graves was staking out Albany Shaker Road, not far from the National Car rental offices in Latham. Earlier in the day, a Teletype message had gone out: be on the lookout for a rented red 1978 Chevrolet with the New York registration 931ZAD. He was waiting to see if it would be returned to the business tonight.

Bingo.

The car, with two men inside, pulled into the rental lot. The officer called for backup. A lieutenant with the last name of Frank arrived and the two approached the car—Frank to the left, Graves to the right.

The officers issued a simple order. "Get out of the car. Slowly."

One of the men, later identified as Webb, eased out of the car. Graves patted him down. In one pocket, the officer found a pair of pliers, lock picks and other tools used to burglarize homes. Webb had rented the car.

Webb was brought to the police station and charged with possession of burglarious tools.

At 8 o'clock that night, Mrs. Truax and her husband were brought to the police station to look at an array of photos to see if they could identify the men who came to their home. Detective R.A. Lynch showed Mrs. Truax ten photos. She picked out two immediately.

"Those are the men who came into my house," she told the detective. The photos were of Ernest J. Thomas and Frank J. Lach, both members of the Fall River Gang.

She looked at a third photograph.

"That looks most like the man who got into the car," she told the detective.

It was a photo of Donald Webb.

Her husband looked at the same array. He picked the same three photos.

Webb was charged with possession of burglarious tools, criminal trespass and attempted burglary in the third degree. At the time of his arrest, he listed his occupation as "clothing salesman" and his address as 9 McCabe Street in Dartmouth, Massachusetts, a modest house.

The three men posted bail, what is essentially a financial promise to return to court.

The Police Department was notified April 25, 1980, that Webb had "jumped bail" and never showed up for court.

A federal warrant for Webb's arrest was issued since Webb was believed to have fled the state. That federal warrant was in effect when Webb, using the alias of his wife's dead husband, was stopped by Chief Adams.

In 1980, learning who was wanted on a fugitive warrant

was a clunky process. Most warrants were not in a central database. Police officers in the field would often radio their station to check on a suspect during a stop and someone there, usually the dispatcher, would then make calls or check any internal records. It was not unusual for someone wanted on a warrant to be stopped by an officer, give a fake name and identification then drive off.

No one was sure what happened the day the Saxonburg Chief stopped Webb. No one was sure why the Chief pulled over the car. No one was sure what words were exchanged. Some speculated Webb was convinced the Chief would discover he was wanted, which led to the violent confrontation. Webb did not want to go back to prison.

One thing was clear, though, when the convict was stopped that December afternoon: Webb was armed.

Webb occasionally carried a small gun on jobs—a .25 Colt, a popular "hideout gun" with gangsters. Some people he worked with didn't like that and stopped going on jobs with him. An armed robbery carried a much longer prison term and they weren't willing to do the additional time, even if the haul was good. Others didn't care.

After jumping bail in New York, Webb and his crew moved south—to Pennsylvania, Virginia and Maryland, investigators would later learn.

But why was Webb in Saxonburg, a small borough in Western Pennsylvania? Some speculated the crew was scoping out the small, family-run jewelry store called Sarvas in town. The downtown store next to a church was also home to the Sarvas family. The business was in the front of the building, the living quarters in the back. If the thieves had hit the store after-hours, the family would likely hear them. No one wanted to think what could have happened if the family confronted the gang. Other investigators believed Webb was just passing through after looking at some larger stores just outside the town.

And how did he slip through a police net dropped so quickly after the Chief was shot? Did someone who lived in the area hide him and help him? If he was injured—as it appeared he was based on the blood found at the scene—how was he able to drive away unnoticed? How could he drive any length of time?

Donald Eugene Webb could not simply vanish.

The differences between Donald Webb and Gregory Blaise Adams were stark. Webb was a career criminal with frayed family ties, educated on the streets, always living on the edge and taking shortcuts in life.

Greg Adams was determined to always do right: get good grades, play sports, go to church, work hard, and commit to family and God. He was quiet, focused and never looking to be the center of attention. Greg believed in that American Dream where hard work and devotion to family paid off with a good life. Good people won in the end. If Donald Webb was the dark criminal lurking in the shadows, Greg Adams was the light chasing it away.

Greg Adams was born at Allegheny Valley Hospital in Natrona Heights, Pennsylvania, one of five children and the only boy born to Ben and Angela Adams. He grew up in farming country in South Buffalo Township in Armstrong County with his sisters. From his grandfather's hillside farm, you could see the banks of the Allegheny River and the unincorporated community of Cadogan in the distance. It was a close-knit, hard-working area of extended relatives, where if anyone yelled someone in the family would answer.

His sisters—Patricia, Maureen, Brenda and Colette—kept a close eye on the baby of the family, this little boy who enthralled them each day.

Greg's maternal grandfather, Angelo Acerni, emigrated from Specchia, Italy, in the 1890s to first work as a "fire boss" in the Kentucky mines, where he examined the mines for explosive dangers, before moving to Pennsylvania. He quickly learned English and became close friends with a neighbor, Pete Bartony, a fellow Italian immigrant, who fixed him up with one of his sisters whom he soon married.

The family lived in a modest farmhouse in South Buffalo

Township and Greg's grandfather worked the farm, in the mines and wide range of jobs to support the family.

One of the Acerni daughters, Angela Grace, married an Irish young man, Benjamin Adams. He was from what was described as a "lace curtain Irish" family. The Adams' four girls and son, Greg, grew up under the eyes of a robust extended family living nearby in South Buffalo Township.

Greg took an early interest in sports. When he was seven or eight, he was given a baseball mitt. "He never took it off," his sister, Patricia Elsenrath, recalled. "He was never seen without it."

When his interest later turned to basketball, his grandfather nailed a bushel basket on the barn so he could shoot hoops, another sister, Colette Sullivan, said.

Eventually, the family moved first to Freeport then Natrona Heights, where Greg's paternal grandparents had lived. Education was important to Greg Adams' family and his parents considered tuition at the local Catholic schools money well spent, even if there wasn't a lot of cash to spend. All of the children went to St. Mary's Grade School, where the Sisters of the Divine Providence taught, and then Blessed Sacrament school.

Greg attended St. Joseph Catholic High School in Natrona Heights for three years before going to Har-Brack High School in Natrona Heights for his senior year, graduating in 1967. The only mention of Greg Adams in his high school yearbook is his senior photo. Dressed in a suit jacket, dress shirt and tie, he is looking pensively off to the right in that standard "studio yearbook" pose of the time.

"He was quiet, very quiet," recalled Jim Watson, who graduated high school with Greg and is the unofficial class historian. Most of the teens hung out at a place called Chuck's where there were dances on Saturday nights. "I never saw him at Chuck's. I never saw him anywhere," Watson recalled.

Greg's sister Patricia said her brother once played point guard on a basketball team during his school years and was remembered as a quiet and studious young man. "He was an all-American boy that you would find in any of the households around us," she said.

He went to Wisconsin State University where he graduated in 1971 with a Bachelor of Science degree in Political Science and spent one summer working at the University of Pittsburgh, staying with his sister Colette Sullivan and her husband, Richard, to save money. His sports interest by this time was tennis (he was once a tennis pro in Butler) and he practiced often.

"All we heard was thump, thump, thump. He was hitting the tennis balls against the garage so he could play better," his brother-in-law, Richard, recalled.

Eventually, Greg Adams left Pennsylvania for a job at the Metropolitan police force in Washington, D.C. where he attended the police academy then worked in patrol, plainclothes and the narcotics divisions beginning in October of 1970, but he felt the pull of home, like beads of metal to a magnet, after he met the woman on the bus who would later become his wife.

When the job in Saxonburg came up, he jumped at it and left Washington in February of 1973. No one was surprised when he returned. His sister Patricia described Western Pennsylvania as the touchstone for those who grew up there. "It is something like the first air you breath. You recognize it as home in your bone marrow," she said.

When Greg returned, he continued to work hard both on the job and in school with laser-like focus. He was a part-time instructor with the Butler County Community College Police Cadet program from January to August of 1974. He earned his graduate degree from Indiana University of Pennsylvania in 1977 and later enrolled in law school. ("He was smart because he worked hard," his sister, Patricia, said.) He withdrew from law school his first semester after he was named Police Chief and his wife was expecting their first child. He wanted to concentrate on his new position and his growing family.

He also taught at the part-time police academy in Seven Springs, which met two days a week, eight hours a day, over the course of nearly a year, and was known for his punctuality and fondness for cowboy boots.

"He started on time and ended on time," recalled W. Joe Hixson, who was in one of Greg's classes. There was just one time he let class out early. "We were shocked. He said the reason was his wife gave birth the day before," Hixson remembered.

Greg also helped out the volunteer fire department at scenes whenever possible, often running the hoses for the firefighters. He was honest, set down firm rules and launched community safety programs in Saxonburg, such as crime watch and identifying valuables in the event of theft for residents. He was skilled in martial arts, played tennis with a competitive edge and, while small, was known for his powerful and swift moves. People remembered him as a no-nonsense man of few words, who would get to the point quickly.

However, family and tradition were what was always important.

After he and Mary Ann married, the couple drove a half hour every Sunday from Saxonburg to South Buffalo Township for dinner with Greg's maternal grandfather, by then a widower, and his aunt, a widow.

Greg Adams was not a man who took shortcuts on the job or in life.

Chapter 4
Coping

Gordon Mainhart pulled out the floor mats and leaned into the Saxonburg police cruiser. For two weeks, he drove a cruiser borrowed from Middlesex Township because the State Police Crime Scene Services technicians were examining the sole Saxonburg police car for evidence. Now, that examination of the cruiser was complete. The car was at the Saxonburg Police station to be put back in service.

This was the first time Gordon had seen the car close-up since December 4. The door was covered with the fine powder used to dust for fingerprints. So was the steering wheel. And the dashboard. And the seats. He expected that.

It was the blood that took him by surprise.

It was spattered on the driver's side door, speckled on the seat, on the floor. Most was caught on the floor. The technicians at the crime lab had examined the cruiser for fingerprints and checked the blood stains—there was enough still left to catch Mainhart's breath—to identify blood types. The floor mats and other pieces of car flooring were taken as evidence.

This was the era before law enforcement and genealogical DNA databases, before a person could be identified through a swab of sweat or a drop of blood. What they could do in 1980 was identify blood types, see if the blood was from more than one person. The technicians would learn blood found at the scene came from two different people. One blood type was the Chief's. The other, Type O, was his killer's. They couldn't tell if the killer's blood came from gunshot wounds, although some people speculated the Chief must have gotten off a shot to wound his killer in the violent struggle.

Gordon wasn't surprised to hear the Chief fought back —and fought hard. Greg Adams was a wiry man. Gordon likened him to a bantam rooster. He was small but tough. Gordon was convinced the Chief would do anything to survive that day. He was heartbroken that it was not enough.

A bucket of soapy water on the ground, Gordon leaned into the cruiser and began to scrub. He scrubbed the cruiser floor, the door, the dashboard. He scrubbed the steering wheel, the seats. As he scrubbed, his vision blurred by fought back tears, he thought of his slain friend, of the Chief's young family left behind, of the shattered innocence of a small town.

It took two days to clean the town's only cruiser.

He would drive it for nearly four more years.

Less than a month after Greg Adams was killed, the lone full-time police officer on the Saxonburg department sat in the meeting room as the borough council met December 29, 1980, in a special session to take a vote.

The council voted unanimously to promote Gordon Mainhart, 26, to Police Chief.

Gordon was solemn as the vote was taken. He thought about Greg Adams in the ambulance, fatally wounded. He felt that aching loss tightening the heart of the community and wondered if it would ever ease.

Gordon didn't have the same educational background or big city police experience as Greg Adams, but he was experienced in different ways and was considered a good pick for Police Chief.

He was raised in nearby Sarver and graduated from Knoch High School in 1973 before joining the U.S. Marine Corps a year later where he served as a military police officer until 1977. He later worked at the U.S. Steel plant in Saxonburg doing security before joining the Saxonburg department full-time in September of 1977. He graduated the Allegheny Police Academy and attended as many additional police seminars as he could.

At another time, he would have been celebrating this new appointment. Instead, in the shadow of the murder, he was draped in this cloak of sadness. He wondered how many people would compare him with Greg? How many would accept any changes he might make, any programs he may start?

He was determined to continue the work Greg Adams started, such as the crime watch program, and he also wanted to make things safer for members of the largely part-time department. The biggest change: officers would not be allowed to leave their cruisers until they called in to the communications center. Any time any vehicle is stopped, registration numbers, locations, descriptions of the people and car or truck needed to be called in before any officer steps out.

For police, a motor vehicle stop is the law enforcement version of "stranger danger." In large cities, calling in vehicle information when a car is pulled over is routine. The officer doesn't know if the driver has a gun, is intoxicated, is mentally ill, or is wanted. The officer doesn't know if the person will fight or flee. The officer is walking up to the unknown.

The report "Death on Patrol: Felonious Homicides of American Police officers" by the Police Foundation found of the 1,916 law enforcement officers killed between 1972 and 1992, 14-percent, or 269, died during a motor vehicle stop. Another 11-percent, or 212, were killed investigating suspicious activities. That same report noted that interviews by the FBI of 51 cop killers indicated most of the killings weren't premeditated: 57-percent of the offenders said they were either surprised or "unprepared" when they committed the murders.

For officers in small communities, such as Saxonburg, there was often a familiarity with those they saw on the road. The drivers they stopped likely were the people they knew: a former classmate, teammate, friend. It might be someone in the next pew at Sunday services. Maybe a relative. In most cases, these stops did not involve the same hyper-vigilance an officer in a large inner city might have.

In 1980, sometimes, when a car was stopped and the officer knew the driver the vehicle information wasn't called in. There didn't seem to be a need. There wasn't a danger. However, the murder of the Chief, one of seven officers killed in Pennsylvania that year, changed the homespun familiarity that blanketed Saxonburg and other small Pennsylvania towns for years. The danger faced by officers in cities such as Philadelphia and Pittsburgh hit home.

In addition to this change in procedure for motor vehicle stops on the Saxonburg department, there would be a personnel change. Gordon would now be working with a new full-time officer, Mark Antoszyk, the brother of the volunteer firefighter who was one of the first on the scene when Greg was killed. Mark had been a part-time officer on another department for several years.

Taking over a department is always difficult, Gordon knew. Taking over from a hero, during a time of inconsolable grief, would be his life challenge. He silently promised Greg he would meet it.

"I just hope people in general will be willing to accept me, not as Greg's substitute, but as my own person," he told a *Butler Eagle* reporter, Debra S. Spisak, at the time.

A few days after Officer Gordon Mainhart became Chief Mainhart, state troopers were packing up the basement command post in the municipal building.

From this post, troopers had coordinated the search first for Stanley Portas then, as the layers of aliases were peeled, for Donald Webb. They checked tips that the accused killer was in Massachusetts, in Virginia, in Rhode Island. They gathered information about the career criminal's associates, where he pulled heists along the East Coast, tried to learn who may be hiding him. They fielded phone calls at the post, gathering tips from the public that often went nowhere.

Now, slightly more than a month after Greg Adams was killed on a road used mainly by locals, the post once manned 24 hours a day, seven days a week, would be shuttered and the investigators moved to the State Police barracks in nearby Butler.

Closing the post made sense. The barracks, less than a half-hour away, provided more services to the investigators. The killer had been identified and was long gone from town. There was nothing left in Saxonburg to investigate. The probe was taking the troopers to other states, to other scenes. Earlier, before Webb was positively identified, they checked out—then ruled out—whether a West Virginia cop killer who escaped a penitentiary in that state could be responsible for the murder. They had traveled to Virginia to track Webb's business and criminal dealings. They staked out places in Massachusetts, where Webb's wife was living. In the months that would follow, they would track leads in Canada, Maine, Florida, and Vermont.

The investigation was still active. It just moved far out of Saxonburg where it all started.

As investigators followed evidentiary breadcrumbs along the East Coast in those days and weeks after the killing, the Saxonburg community and relatives of the Adams children looked closer to home to bring a sense of normalcy for the boys. Someone brought in a small Christmas tree to the Adams home and decorated it. A small party was hosted to celebrate Ben's third birthday.

After a death, the cliché "life goes on" is often repeated. It doesn't matter how heart-wrenching the loss, the day-to-day work of living never ends. Mary Ann now knew this well. She had two boys to raise, bills to pay, a house to run. She still got up in the middle of the night as needed to soothe either Ben or her infant son, Greg. She still needed to cook breakfast, lunch and dinner. She still needed to change diapers and do laundry. She still needed to continue the tasks of life. Now, she would be doing it all without Greg.

She felt the warmth and generosity of the townspeople of Saxonburg. She was grateful for help offered without her asking. Townspeople raised money for the family and the children's future education. People were so eager to assist, to help shoulder the grief in any way possible. But the pain of losing her husband, the father of her boys, was hers alone.

The leads quickly went cold in the month after Greg Adams was killed. That was what surprised the Pennsylvania troopers the most. It was as if they were in the midst of a magical act where the performer steps into a closed box onstage then, with the wave of the wand, is gone when it is opened.

The troopers kept looking for the escape door, the deflecting mirrors, the slight of hand source and, each time, came up short. Investigators kept following Webb's wife and friends. They kept going back to people with even the most tenuous ties to Webb. Family. Friends of family. Neighbors. People locked up in jails and prisons along the East Coast. People on parole. Crede and the other investigators felt they were close to finding Webb but clearly not close enough. A killer could not just vanish. Could he?

By mid-January of 1981, with no sign of Donald Webb in Massachusetts, the Pennsylvania state troopers were reluctantly called back home. The FBI agents in the New Bedford office and the Massachusetts State Police unit assigned to the Bristol County District Attorney's Office planned to keep watching Lillian—and her house—for any signs of Webb and would follow up leads in Massachusetts.

Almost simultaneously that month, the case also changed hands in the FBI Massachusetts office when FBI Agent George Bates was transferred to New Orleans to work on other cases, a transfer in the works well before the murder. While he would eventually return to work in the FBI fugitive unit in Massachusetts, the day-to-day investigation was assigned to fellow agent, Jack McGraw. Jack was a close friend and George knew, while he was in New Orleans, the two would be talking quite a bit by phone about the case, even if they weren't working side-by-side. It was a smooth transition, both men said.

On May 4, 1981, five months after the murder, Webb was

placed on the FBI's *10 Most Wanted Fugitive List.* The wanted poster was tacked in post offices and police departments
across the country and garnered headlines in Pennsylvania.
But the inclusion rated barely a mention in the newspapers in
Massachusetts, the state where Webb once lived and had the
strongest ties.

The Herald News of Fall River, nearly two weeks after the
killer was added to the list, ran a two-column, seven-para-
graph story and Webb's front and side mug shots on page 5 of
its May 16 edition, noting the FBI announced Webb might be
in the Fall River-New Bedford area.

The headline read: "On FBI list." The article was squeezed
above a story about the Boys and Girls Club accepting camp
applications and next to a syndicated health column. The story
was roughly the same size as the ad on the page for the Sunday
special of roast lamb at Magoni's Restaurant in an adjoining
town. It was the first time there was mention in that city's paper that police were looking for the fugitive.

In Taunton, where Webb once lived, and in New Bedford,
where his wife called home, there were no articles or photos
about his addition to the national most wanted list in May
1981. It wasn't until July 3, 1981, that a story and mug shot appeared on page 4 in the New Bedford paper, noting Webb was
seen in Fall River two weeks earlier.

Lawrence Gilligan, Special Agent in the FBI Boston office, told the paper the bureau received reports from reliable
sources that Webb was "definitely" seen in Fall River and that
the bureau believed the suspect was still in the Fall River-New
Bedford area.

"He was born in Oklahoma City but he has spent most of
his life in Southeastern Massachusetts," Gilligan told the New
Bedford paper.

One member of the Massachusetts State Police, Paul
Fitzgerald, later recalled the lack of widespread publicity as
stunning and unsettling. "It was amazing nothing was brought
up," he said. "It was beyond belief … There was minimal to
nothing in the media."

A former New Bedford detective, Gardner Greany, also

remembered how everyone in local law enforcement knew the fugitive was likely in the area and found it odd there was so little publicity. Why that was remained unclear. It could have been because there were at least three separate law enforcement agencies involved, with each deferring to the other. It could have been because dealing with reporters at the time was not a high priority. It could have been because prosecutors and some detectives in the Bristol County District Attorney's Office were tied up in several high profile cases, including the investigation of a Taunton nurse accused of killing her patients (she was later acquitted) and the so-called "Fall River cult murder" case riveting the area where three women were discovered killed between 1979 and 1980. (Some of the troopers in the prosecutor's small unit handling those cases were required to be in court to testify in either pre-trial hearings or for the trials, draining any state police manpower for extra searches.)

No one, years later, could remember why it happened. Those deep in the hunt would later say they were laser focused on finding Webb, not drawing more media attention. However, the physical and psychological divide between New Bedford and Fall River didn't help.

At the time, the Fall River and New Bedford areas were considered worlds unto their own. The parochialism of New England was deeply rooted and many living in the two municipalities didn't venture far beyond the city limits. For some it was a matter of economic practicality—they didn't have cars and walked or took a bus to get around.

They lived in the city, often in neat, three-family houses peopled by extended relatives, and worked in the city. Families immigrated across oceans, taking root in the community and often never ventured away.

Outside the circle of what was known as Southeastern Massachusetts, before the more fashionable description "south coast" took hold decades later giving the mill towns an upscale flair, most in Boston considered the area too far to draw much notice. It was, to Boston-area politicians, the end of the universe. Tiny Rhode Island was even more provincial than

New Bedford and Fall River. Driving out of the state was an excursion for many, even though Massachusetts shared a border.

Once a Fall River detective after catching a wanted suspect in Tiverton, Rhode Island, a then rural community bordering the city, joked the man thought he was eluding capture because he considered Rhode Island another country. Even those living in New Bedford or Fall River stayed close to home. It was a 30-minute drive between the two along Route 6, the secondary highway peppered with stoplights, or a slightly shorter ride on Interstate 195.

The cities were similar on one level: hard-working first and second generation immigrants from Portugal, Ireland, and Canada, many working in the textile mills or other factories. But there was a divide between the two communities.

Fall River was a city of confusing one-way streets with an under-utilized waterfront, its historical claim to fame Lizzie Borden, the woman acquitted in the 1892 axe murder of her father and stepmother and the childhood rhyme immortalizing it: "Lizzie Borden took an axe and gave her mother 40 whacks. When she saw what she had done, she gave her father 41."

New Bedford was a city of the sea, its working waterfront at the base of a hill where sea captains once lived. It was known as the setting for the novel Moby Dick as well as one of the stops on the Underground Railroad during the times of slavery (New Bedford was home to 300 to 700 escaped slaves by the 1840s, the National Park Service notes). The narrow and long city – someone once wryly noted it looked like Manhattan upended– was easy to maneuver with its main and busy streets connecting cramped neighborhoods.

The two newspapers in the cities at the time reflected the perception of residents in the communities, which kept the publications' circulation circles tight. Rarely did the Fall River newspaper carry New Bedford news. The New Bedford newspaper, considered at the time the more aggressive publication of the two, saved the bulk of Fall River news for its Sunday "Fall River edition" because *The Herald News* didn't publish on Sundays at the time.

"New Bedford and Fall River had that little scope view of the world at the time," Fitzgerald said. "It was that thinking: 'If it didn't happen here, it isn't important.'"

As a result, in those pre-internet and social media days, there was no mention in the local Massachusetts papers of the stakeouts by police, of the Pennsylvania State Police troopers' weeks-long stay or the FBI and Pennsylvania coordination of the multi-state search. Of course, during the first days after Webb was identified and before the arrest warrant was issued in late December of 1980, investigators wanted to keep the Massachusetts search out of the public light as long as possible, fearing Webb would go deeper underground.

They wanted Webb to let his guard down, even though it was clear he knew he was wanted thanks to information given to his wife by a Massachusetts State Police Captain. The focus at the time, several said, was tracking leads and catching Webb. However, members of the local law enforcement community still knew Webb was wanted. The information was read at roll call at the start of local police shifts.

Webb's stepson, who was a police cadet for five years and later became a New Bedford police officer in May 1980, was at those roll calls in the city's North End station, recalled retired New Bedford detective Gardner Greany, who as a patrol officer worked the same shift as the younger Webb. FBI Agent George Bates said the stepson was also questioned about the fugitive's whereabouts. (Stanley Webb was later "discharged" from the police department on October 26, 1983. He later told a reporter he quit.) Donald Webb was not an unknown in the city. Some of the officers, particularly those in New Bedford and Fall River, could recognize him on sight.

However, New Bedford Police Department officers were not actively involved in the search for the suspect and not part of the FBI and State Police efforts. Part of that may have been because Stanley Webb's position on the force and fears that somehow the killer could be tipped off yet again, either inadvertently or deliberately, about the search efforts.

But even after Webb was listed on the FBI Most Wanted List, the general public in the Greater New Bedford-Fall River area was unaware Webb, an accused killer with a wife living nearby, was on the loose. If a reporter had asked, one investigator said, authorities would have told them about the warrant but no one in law enforcement recalls anyone from local papers asking about the suspect at the time. And no one offered up the information. This meant members of the community might have seen a man matching Webb's description, unaware he was wanted. Today, more eyes on the street translate into cases solved, as Amber Alerts issued for abducted children repeatedly show.

Police now actively interact with the public on social media looking for tips on identifying suspects and the whereabouts of fugitives. But the early 1980s represented a different time in law enforcement practices. In some cases, there was fear the release of too much information to the public would harm a case, allowing suspects to escape apprehension. The less the public knew, the less the suspects knew. There were also fewer individuals designated as "public relations" officials in law enforcement.

There was the feeling by some that it was up to reporters to dig out information, to at least ask. Everyone had a job and those jobs didn't always blend well.

So, as the manhunt for the cop killer continued in 1981, the public in Southeastern Massachusetts was largely oblivious. The community was left with short stories, buried deep in a newspaper, of a New Bedford man wanted for murder in Pennsylvania, and wanted posters in post offices. The FBI Wanted poster featured Webb's photo, his description and the type of legitimate jobs he held over the years, such as butcher, salesman, and vending machine repairman.

How many people in Massachusetts took notice of the posters or the brief news stories remained unclear. The lack of publicity led to later speculation that someone in law enforcement didn't want Webb found. One theory was that Webb was an informant, something investigators would later deny. What this hunt out of the public view likely did was create an atmosphere of missed opportunities. How do you find someone if no one in the public is looking?

In the years after the killing, there were also internal changes in the Massachusetts State Police unit assigned to the Bristol County District Attorney's Office that could have disrupted the search. In the September 1982 Democratic election primary, District Attorney Ronald A. Pina beat challenger Patrick E. Lowney, a Fall River attorney and the brother of State Police Sgt. Dan Lowney who was working the case.

Many of the troopers working in Pina's office were supporting Dan's brother and, two days after the winner-take-all primary (no Republicans were running in the highly Democratic region), the District Attorney kicked all of the troopers out of his downtown New Bedford building.

"They were out to get me," Pina was quoted at the time in the *Standard-Times* of New Bedford newspaper. "They lost."

The troopers assigned to the District Attorney's investigative unit, handling cases in the county ranging from murder to drug trafficking, technically answered to the State Police brass in Boston. In reality, they were caught between two bosses—one elected, the other a quasi-military law enforcement agency—and walked carefully between the two.

The Massachusetts troopers tracking Webb were now housed in the State Police barracks in Dartmouth one town over. Those troopers eventually transferred to different investigative or uniform units in the state, their slots in the unit assigned to the Bristol County District Attorney's Office replaced by others. One trooper who left just before the purge, Paul Fitzgerald, said he didn't think the ouster affected the search for Webb because it wasn't a local case under the DA's direction.

"It was a Mass. State Police, Pennsylvania State Police and FBI case," he later recalled.

Between politics and job transfers, the two years that followed the killing were frustrating for the investigators trying to stay on point. In Massachusetts, much of the work was now left to the FBI. Those federal agents, as were state troopers in both Massachusetts and Pennsylvania, were convinced Lillian Webb knew where her husband was. The key was getting her to talk.

FBI Agent Bates, and later his colleague McGraw, tried unsuccessfully to convince prosecutors to let them search her New Bedford house. No, they were repeatedly told. There were no legal grounds, no legal probable cause, to do it. To get it, they needed some evidence, other than a hunch, that Webb was hiding in the house. They didn't have it.

So, the agents kept following her. They searched through trash. They interviewed neighbors. They checked financial records. They examined phone records. And they kept knocking on Lillian's door, asking her a simple question: "Where is Donald Webb?"

The answer was always the same. "I don't know."

The evidence to obtain a search warrant for Lillian's house eluded the agents.

What they did have was a lot of frustration.

What they would not do, what they could not do, was give up hope.

The gun was just laying there, about 20 feet from the road in Pennsylvania's Winfield Township in Butler County near a snow fence when the two boys walking home from school first spotted it. The April temperatures in 1981 hovered in the 40s, sometimes hitting 60, and the snow covering the ground was melting, revealing all that had been beneath it.

Cornplanter Road, where the two boys were, is a rural and sometimes winding road, about seven miles from Saxonburg. There are farms and homes surrounded by acres of land. There wasn't much traffic along the road, mostly residents driving home and a few trucks either delivering supplies or picking up farm items. This was a place off the beaten path in an era before GPS mapping apps cooed directions. It was a place you knew or stumbled across while lost.

The school bus passed the spot five days a week when classes were in session. Students walked by the spot twice a day, going to and leaving the bus stop. But in the winter snow, no one could see the .38 caliber handgun likely flung from a car in December.

It took the spring thaw to uncover what was later identified as Police Chief Greg Adams' service weapon. The gun, exposed to four months of weather, was now rusted and all six rounds had been fired.

Along this same road, four years and two months later on February 22, 1985, an eight-year-old girl named Cherrie Mahan, wearing brown Cabbage Patch earmuffs and carrying a blue backpack, would hop off her school bus around 4 p.m. and head toward her home 100 yards away.

She never made it to her house. There were no footprints in the snow in her driveway. Students on the bus later told police they saw a light blue Dodge van parked nearby with mountain or ski scene painted on it. (In 2020, the child remained missing and it remained an active, although cold, case.)

People in close communities don't forget the lost. The hurt and horror knits into the pearls of life, the memory blended with the present. For decades, the killing of Chief Gregory Adams and the later disappearance of Cherrie Mahan would haunt residents in Saxonburg and the surrounding semi-rural communities. Two horrific crimes unanswered, shattering the innocence of small town America.

Around the time the Chief's gun was found in April, Lillian Webb was officially moving from her apartment on Carriage Drive in New Bedford to a house on Hawthorne Street in the same city. If Carriage Drive was tough to stake out, this new residence was a logistical nightmare. The street was fairly busy and there was no place to park.

Massachusetts State Police Sgt. Dan Lowney and others spent hours driving along Hawthorne Street, looking for a good spot to watch the house. There wasn't one, they discovered. Circling the area also drew attention. When neighbors saw the undercover police cars, they called the New Bedford Police Department to report a suspicious vehicle fearing a burglar was staking out the area.

Following Lillian was an even greater challenge. Each time of the many times investigators tried to tail her, they quickly discovered they had been "made." She seemed to have an innate ability to spot anyone who tried to follow her and she always knew the best way to elude a tail. She circled neighborhoods, made sharp turns, took long drives before circling back home. They were all the things investigators described in later reports as classic "evasive measures."

Confronting her at her house also failed. Each time investigators came to the door, she insisted she didn't know where Donald was. Occasionally, she let them inside to tell them. Often, though, she just kept them on the stoop.

Her neighbors were cooperative but had little information to offer. No one had seen Webb at the house. Even those who could see into the backyard of the Webb house from their own second-floor windows reported nothing suspicious and saw no one matching Webb's description in the area.

But the troopers and FBI agents were still convinced Lillian knew something. They kept following her. They kept the house under watch. Once, they traced a call made to Lillian from a motel pay phone in a town near Fall River, Massachusetts. FBI and state police rushed to the area a half-hour from Lillian's home. When they got there, there was no sign of Donald Webb.

The tears came in the quiet of the night, when the children were asleep, when the daily tasks of laundry, cooking, grocery shopping were complete, when the lights were out and the darkness filled the room. It was then that wall of strength crumpled. It was then Mary Ann Adams, alone in her room, felt the empty place in her heart and cried. She made sure the children never saw those tears that first year after Greg's death, or the years that followed. She wiped them quickly away at Sunday Mass when the soloist's voice echoed through the church, when the songs harkened her back to the funeral.

For her, life was now split: before Greg's murder and after.

In that blur of year one without Greg, Mary Ann crafted plans in the short-term. In the beginning it was hour-by-hour.

The wake, the funeral, all the other practical details a family attends to after a death. She took baby steps adjusting at first. Soon, she planned a day ahead; then, by the end of that year, a week. She relied heavily on a calendar but sometimes even that failed her. Once, she made two appointments for each of the boys on the same day and time in different places.

The simple holidays, Fourth of July, Memorial Day, a birthday, were painful. She found herself thinking back to when Greg was there. She thought about what he was missing. She would feel her eyes mist and she would blink the grief back. She would look, instead, at her boys. Her gifts from Greg. Her anchors.

In 1981, the first year "after," Lady Diana Spencer married Charles, the Prince of Wales. The space shuttle Columbia was launched. The first American test tube baby was born. *The Raiders of the Lost Ark* hit the theaters. "Bette Davis Eyes" by Kim Carnes was at the top of the Billboard charts. The police television series *Hill Street Blues* premiered on NBC. Ronald Reagan was inaugurated as president. The 52 hostages held in the American embassy in Iran were freed. The Pope was shot. Mary Ann recalls little of what went on outside her world in Saxonburg. Those days were a blur of getting the children fed and clothed, of protecting them, of crying in private, of trying to stay strong.

Eventually, she returned to work after a year. At first it was part-time in computer operations at Du-Co Ceramics, then she took a job at an insurance company before joining the school district as a secretary.

Over the years, she would accept honors in her husband's name and attend memorials in his honor. Sometimes the children—although often, it was just Ben those first years—would attend, such as when she received a medal and certificate from the American Police Hall of Fame in Greg's memory a month after the killing. Dozens, and sometimes more than 100, Saxonburg residents would come out to mark the yearly anniversaries of his death.

The town erected a memorial etched with the Chief's image in front of the Municipal Building. When a federal program was signed into law by President Bill Clinton in 1998, providing $25 million yearly for three years to help buy bullet-proof vests, she was at a local ceremony with both boys—then grown. Pennsylvania U.S. Rep. Ron Klink, who as a television reporter in 1980 covered the murder, spearheaded the original bill.

She stayed in Saxonburg for eight years after the shooting, keeping in close touch with her late husband's family, before finally moving on to nearby Cabot less than three miles away. But in those first months and years, her focus was on her boys. She left the investigation in the hands of the police. If there was an update, she knew they would call. When an arrest was made, she would be in court to see the killer. Until then, she let the police do their work and she spent her days and weeks doing hers as a mother.

Chapter 5
Haunted

The Roman lyric poet Horace once wrote that time will bring to light whatever is hidden. For the original investigators in the murder case, it seemed to bring little more than shifting shadows as years passed. Those who initially worked the case eventually were promoted or moved into other units but the killing of Gregory Adams unsettled them all. They couldn't let it go completely.

FBI Agent George Bates was one of those people. He was relieved when he finally returned from New Orleans to Massachusetts in 1983 to work in the agency's fugitive unit in Boston. He was eager to resume working on the case that never left his mind.

In the period he was gone, he regularly spoke with fellow agents McGraw, who was now handling the investigation in Massachusetts, and Pete McCann in Pennsylvania and stayed up-to-date on developments. To the agents, the case was paradoxical. Based on everything they knew, everything they did, Donald Eugene Webb should theoretically have been captured by now.

The shreds of evidence, stitched together rapidly in the hours and days after the killing thanks to the persistence of those first Pennsylvania state troopers, provided the killer's name. It lead to Massachusetts. It lead to a car rental business in Taunton, Massachusetts. It was supposed to lead them directly to the killer.

That December 1980 day when Bates talked to the clerk at the car rental place and learned the killer stayed at a nearby hotel, he and others were convinced the suspect's days on the run were coming to a close. But days turned to weeks to months and years.

The trail Webb left after the shooting—from Pennsylvania straight to Southeastern Massachusetts—stopped quickly. Call it investigative instinct or just plain field experience, Bates was convinced the key to finding the killer lay in one city and one person: New Bedford, Massachusetts and Webb's wife. In some investigations you follow the money. In others, you follow those closest to the target. In the search for Donald Eugene Webb, a man with few roots, Bates knew they needed to do both and more.

George Bates wasn't the only person surprised Webb was still a fugitive. In that first month after the killing, when State Police and the FBI seemed so close to catching Webb, Pennsylvania Trooper Jim Poydence could see, in his mind's eye, Webb sitting in a courtroom, at the defense table, as jurors listened to witnesses in the murder trial.

Then, after weighing the evidence, the 12 members of that jury would file into the hushed courtroom. It would likely be a short deliberation. The jury foreman or forewoman would hand up the verdict slip, then, in a clear voice, say one word: guilty. That was how it was supposed to end. Life does not always turn out the way it should. That trail to the trial, once so direct, so clear, was now a labyrinth in the fog.

Time is rarely a friend to either a murder investigation or a search for a fugitive. They all knew chances of finding Webb diminished with each day, week, month, and year. The fugitive had more time to hide, to cover his mistakes, his tracks, his identity. They knew all this but still held out hope. The slaying of Chief Adams still hung over the community of Saxonburg, haunting the borough and gnawing at the soul of law enforcement officers and their families in Western Pennsylvania. If it could happen in Saxonburg, a gentle community without malice, it could happen anywhere.

However, as months turned to years with no sign of the killer, the belief that Webb would be found began to diminish. Jim Poydence, though, was still hopeful. He was not a quitter.

That was why, on July 13, 1983, nearly three years after the murder, Poydence was upbeat getting off the plane with a Pennsylvania prosecutor in Providence. The two were to attend a two-day conference with FBI agents on the case but flew in a day early expecting to talk with Lillian Webb, the fugitive's wife. It was something investigators had tried to do since December of 1980 with little success. Every time a FBI agent went to her door, asking where Donald was, her answer was simple: "I don't know." Sometimes, there was a slight variation: "I have nothing to say."

But this time appeared to be different. The investigators called her well-known attorney, John F. Cicilline, who once represented the notorious Rhode Island mob boss, Raymond L.S. Patriarca, and made arrangements to meet in his office to talk with the woman. *This could be the turning point,* Poydence thought. *This could close the case.*

It wasn't easy dealing with Lillian. She made it clear she didn't want to talk to investigators about her husband. She also knew they were watching her. When she pulled into her garage, the automatic door closed just as the rear bumper cleared. When she pulled out, her car was already running. When law enforcement officers picked through the curbside trash outside her home, there was no sign Donald or even a second person was living with her.

When authorities followed Lillian, she would make sharp turns down neighborhood streets to lose them. They never saw a second person in the car. They never saw a second person in the windows of the house. They never saw a sign of Donald Eugene Webb. If Lillian was hiding him, she was doing a good job. She was smart and shrewd and tough, they concluded. Most of all, she appeared to be loyal to her husband.

Jim Poydence flew into Providence with prosecutor David Cook and met up with Rhode Island State Police Lt. Charles Cunningham on that July 1983 day. The trio then drove to the attorney's office for a pre-arranged 10 a.m. appointment with the defense attorney. This was it. Finally. A face-to-face in a lawyer's office, he felt, meant one thing: cooperation and a deal. They would finally get Donald Eugene Webb.

At least that was the plan. The investigators asked if the attorney could arrange a meeting with Lillian. The meeting was set for 1:30 that afternoon.

One step closer, Jim thought.

If Lillian didn't plan to cooperate, she wouldn't agree to meet with them, Jim thought. This was a good sign.

When Lillian finally arrived to the first floor office, the troopers and the prosecutor introduced themselves and formally let her know why they were there.

"Mrs. Webb, we would like to interview you about your husband," Poydence told her.

"My attorney has advised me not to say anything," she answered, Poydence recalled.

The troopers and the prosecutor stared at her and, stewing, walked out of the office. The Rhode Island lieutenant dropped off Poydence and Cook at the Old Hotel Providence where they spent the night before the conference the next day. They were now sure of one thing: Lillian Webb, if she knew anything, would never talk.

After that frustrating meeting, FBI agents and Pennsylvania state police investigators gathered for two days in Providence, Rhode Island to talk about the case. At that "Webb Conference" on July 14 and 15, 1983, the investigators critiqued and catalogued the leads, reviewed files and looked for ways to convince people to provide information about the killer.

Agent Bates, who was at the meeting with fellow agent Pete McCann, talked about what appeared to be a credible lead from an informant they had followed up on a year earlier, in May 1982. The informant, who was usually reliable and knew Webb fairly well, said Webb was supposed to be in Miami with his friend Frank J. Lach, a member of the Fall River burglary crew. Agents had been advised that "Lach is considered (a) key person in the future apprehension of Webb since December 1980 for consideration of Federal Harboring Statute," one FBI report noted.

In the weeks and months prior, according to FBI files, agents examined records from public pay phones and private phones in places such as the main waiting room at Grand Central Station in New York, a pay phone at the Howard Johnson restaurant in Blandford, Massachusetts, locations in Plainfield, Connecticut and Newtown, Connecticut.

The investigation, though, was leading investigators to Florida as agents looked to those who knew Webb and Lach for additional leads. The FBI obtained toll call records for two people, covering the time period of October 19, 1981, to April 8, 1982. The records revealed 15 short calls between October 22, 1981, to April 5, 1982, originating in North Dade, Florida. There were calls on October 22 and 23, 1981 from Hollywood, Florida. There was a collect call on March 11, 1982.

Then, a Rhode Island mobster and tipster with ties to Webb and Lach bolstered the possibility that the pair was in Florida. According to FBI records, Frank A. Vendituoli was interviewed at Squires Restaurant in Barrington, Rhode Island on May 5, 1982. At the time, Vendituoli still had a year to go on his federal probation and was told he would shortly be indicted on charges of violating banking laws. At that meeting, Vendituoli said he believed Webb, Lach and a third man were together, "probably living in the Florida area and traveling on the East Coast to do jewelry burglaries with a fourth person doing the alarm work."

Bates eventually received additional information that Webb and Lach would be at a pawn shop on a specific day to sell some stolen items.

There was a hitch, of course. There always was. Bates and the investigators working directly on the case were in New England and Pennsylvania. They needed to rely on their counterparts in Miami, agents they didn't know well. Bates wanted to make sure nothing went sideways.

Bates later said he gave the Miami FBI office specific and firm instructions: Webb will be with Lach who was wanted for unlawful flight to avoid prosecution in connection with a New York burglary. Don't arrest him. We can always get him another time. We want Webb. He is our priority.

Lach was well known to law enforcement and was featured that month in month in the FBI Law Enforcement Bulletin magazine. He was wanted for interstate flight after a federal warrant was issued for his arrest on the New York charges where he and Webb posed as sewer inspectors. He had that tough guy look straight out of central casting. He was a big guy: six foot tall, between 240 and 270 pounds and described by the FBI as "heavy, fat."

In a 1978 photo, the balding Lach is staring straight at the camera, an image of someone you don't mess with. His occupations, when he wasn't in jail or stealing, included working as a butcher, plasterer, salesman and pizza parlor manager. It was noted in the bulletin that Lach might be with Donald Eugene Webb, one of the Ten Most Wanted. Both men were considered armed, dangerous and escape risks, the FBI Bulletin noted. However, to those who arrested Lach in the past, he wasn't known as dangerous. He was a career criminal, a thief. The alert for Lach was another avenue in the search for Webb.

The operation in Miami needed strict rules, Bates knew. If Lach was arrested first, Bates was convinced Webb, if he were there, would slip away—making it even harder to find him. Getting Lach to cooperate once caught was unlikely. The mission was to get Webb. That is why Bates repeated the instructions on the phone to fellow agents in Florida. "Get Webb first. Do not arrest Lach if you don't have Webb. Got it?"

Then Bates waited.

When the call from Miami came on May 13, 1982, the agent on the other end was elated.

"We got him. We got him," the Miami agent said, Bates recalled. "We got Lach."

Bates, who was convinced the original tip was solid, felt the frustration rise. If Webb was in Miami, there was no way he would stay in town after the arrest of his buddy. Webb would know, or suspect, he was the target.

Frank Lach, dubbed a "professional criminal" by an FBI spokesman at the time of his arrest, gave authorities the alias "Armand Joseph Dinofrio" when arrested and, according to an FBI, "refused to make any statements whatsoever." He was driving a $40,000 Cadillac, paid for in cash, and was wearing an $8,000 wristwatch. His fingerprints revealed his real name. He was arrested on a fugitive from justice warrant in connection with the same Colonie, New York burglary Webb was wanted on at the time of the Chief's murder.

Lach, who was held at the Dade County Jail in Miami, was eventually sent back to New York where he was later convicted and sentenced to three-and-a-half to seven years in prison. (He was paroled in 1985 but arrested again a year later on a charge of Interstate transportation of stolen property)

Bates later heard a rumor about how close they had come to catching Webb in Miami. Webb was in a business nearby and saw authorities surround Lach's car, he was told. As Lach left in handcuffs, Webb simply turned and walked away. Vanished yet again.

No one was certain if that story was true. No one could officially confirm Webb was in Miami and Lach wasn't talking. Years later, other investigators came to doubt the veracity of that tip, wondering if the informant was feeding bogus information to cut a deal in another case. It was yet another tale surrounding the man they were now dubbing The Ghost.

When "friends" of the accused killer were arrested—and not surprisingly it happened often—they would, like the informant with the Miami tip, tell tales of where Donald Eugene Webb was, hoping to cut official or unofficial deals with police or prosecutors. Those who knew nothing talked. Those who might know were silent. Many people, though, pointed investigators in a single general direction: Massachusetts.

That was what happened when one of Webb's Fall River Gang friends, the "alarm guy" named David Hutchins, was locked up in Williamsport, Pennsylvania, on a foiled jewelry heist in that community. He told Pennsylvania State Police on February 21, 1981, that he believed the suspect was in the New Bedford, Massachusetts area. He insisted Webb's wife knew where he was.

Jim Poydence knew about Hutchins' statements as he waited in the holding area to talk with another prisoner at a New York prison with a New York State Police officer, Jack Brandt, in 1982, one year before that failed meeting with Lillian. He didn't expect to get too much but they had to give it a shot. Frank Lach, one of Webb's pals, who was caught in Miami a couple of months earlier in 1982, was pretty tight with Webb. If anyone might know where the fugitive was, Lach would. He was being held awaiting trial on the attempted heist in Colonie, New York he committed with Webb not long before the Chief was killed. Jim hoped the guy, now facing more charges, would talk.

Lach walked through the doorway, escorted by a correction officer, and looked at the investigators.

"Where are you from?" Lach asked, Poydence recalled.

"We want to talk to you about Donald Webb," the Pennsylvania trooper answered.

Lach turned around. "Take me back to my cell," he told the correction officer, Poydence recalled.

It was a scene repeated in other prisons in other states with other inmates as investigators tried to convince the men once close to Webb to cooperate. No one was sure if it was loyalty to a criminal colleague or just empty bravado.

Sometimes, though, someone would provide information so detailed that investigators were convinced the search was ending. That was what the investigators thought in 1984 when they heard Webb was in Canada.

There had been many "sightings" of Webb across the country since the Police Chief's killing. Webb was in Puerto Rico, in Miami, in New York. There was the man in San Antonio, Texas, who looked like Webb. There was the report that Webb was on a cruise ship. Yet another report that he was dead. But the tip from a mobster in Massachusetts that the killer was in Canada appeared to be the most credible.

The informant was plugged into the Providence mob and, when he got jammed up, shared tidbits with law enforcement in Massachusetts and Rhode Island. Massachusetts State Police

Sgt. Dan Lowney had dealt with the guy for years and, while never totally trusting him, knew he often had good information. The key, Dan knew, was to remember the guy always had an ulterior not altruistic motive.

Dan, one of the state troopers booted from the Bristol County District Attorney's building after the 1982 election, took notice when the informant told him in August of 1984 that Webb was in or would be in Canada. The informant could meet him there, Dan was told.

A contingent of Pennsylvania state troopers and a prosecutor flew to New England on August 16, 1984, to meet up with FBI agents as well as members of the Massachusetts and Rhode Island state police. From there, they drove to Newport, Vermont, about ten miles from the Canadian border and checked into the Newport City Motel.

While they were in Vermont, the informant was driving to Canada with Fall River Detective Paul Carey, Jr. The car was furnished by law enforcement, the Fall River detective recalled. So was the roughly $1,800 for expenses, Carey said. The destination was the Blue Bonnet racetrack where the informant insisted Webb would be. Carey and the informant first checked into a Montreal hotel—"a real nice one," Carey later said. The next day, Carey and the informant went to the racetrack and the law enforcement officers drove to the Royal Canadian Mounted Police (RCMP) headquarters.

Then things broke down.

The head of the RCMP investigative division told the Americans his people would take it from there. After all, they were on Canadian soil and Canadian law enforcement officers had jurisdiction now. If Webb showed up, a team would be sent out to take him into custody

"Gentlemen, you have to understand, you are in a different country," he said, Pennsylvania Trooper Jim Poydence and Lowney recalled.

The American investigators weren't pleased but were still hopeful it would work out. So, they waited that day for the call from the informant about meeting Webb. And they waited. And waited.

The next day, the call came.

Things didn't go as planned. The informant blew all the money at the track and Webb never showed up.

The investigators drove back home.

So did the informant.

The Fall River detective years later said he was convinced the informant made the whole thing up. "It was a scam," Carey recalled.

The news cycle moves quickly. That was true even before the continuous blast of "breaking news" headlines on cable news stations and the internet. Even that era where newsprint ruled and listeners tuned to local television stations at six and 11, when people could pause to soak in the intricacies of an issue, the public eventually moved on to other topics. Other stories graced the front pages of the Pennsylvania daily newspapers and the television and radio airwaves as the years passed, except for an occasional story about a memorial service marking the death of Saxonburg Chief Greg Adams. The public spotlight seemed to fade outside the footprint of the borough and those who remembered him.

The new Saxonburg Police Chief, Gordon Mainhart, feared, as the decades passed, as new people moved into town, even if the killer was found, there would be people in Saxonburg who never knew Greg Adams. Some would be born decades after his death. Some would even be on the Saxonburg force. It was important to keep the memory alive, Gordon knew, especially for those on the department. He decided in 1984 to create a new Saxonburg police patch in honor of Greg for the department's uniforms.

The 4½ by 3½ patch, designed by Mainhart, was simple. The background was black, except for the center circle in gold. It incorporated the history of the borough with the police department name. In an inner circle was the Brooklyn Bridge, a nod to the town's co-founder who designed the span using his patented wire rope cable system. The next circle read, "Butler County, PA" with two oak leaf clusters on either side. The outer circle read Saxonburg Police in white block letters. Each patch by the Eastern Emblem Manufacturing Corp. would cost $2.78.

The Mayor, Reldon W. Cooper, approved the patch design in September of 1984. It was dedicated and placed in service on December 4, 1984, in honor of Greg Adams. It was one of the many memorials to the slain Chief in town. It was the one that kept Greg Adams on the job, always watching over the department, Mainhart felt.

In 1987, Jim Poydence moved up the ranks on the Pennsylvania State Police and out of the criminal investigation unit in Butler. As a new corporal, he was the patrol supervisor in a small, state police station in McConnellsburg in the mountains of Fulton County. He expected the transfer. Just about everybody promoted to corporal worked patrol for a year. After that, he would join another unit in Pittsburgh, first investigating fraud then organized crime before retiring in 1996. But the murder of Chief Greg Adams never left him. New investigators still called, asking for advice. Copies of his notes from the case and personal files were meticulously kept, a constant reminder of justice long unserved.

The man who took over the unit from Poydence in 1987 was a trooper named Danny McKnight who worked out of the Butler barracks. McKnight remembered clearly the dragnet set the day Chief Adams was killed, how troopers throughout the region searched the highways for the getaway car and local motels for the suspect. He was on the road that day, checking for speeders, and was quickly drawn into the hunt.

McKnight knew how exhaustive the investigation had been since 1980. He, like others, was convinced the killer was long gone from Pennsylvania and the best leads would come from other states. Seven years after the murder, something new had to be done.

It took awhile to make it happen, but he and others eventually convinced a national television program to spotlight the case.

Gordon Mainhart stood by the Agway store parking lot on Butler Street, behind the camera crews, and watched the crew set up the scene in May of 1989. The television show, *America's Most Wanted* hosted by John Walsh, was doing a segment on Greg Adams' murder. It had been nearly nine years since an arrest warrant for Donald Eugene Webb was issued and the investigators were hoping the show could provide leads to where the accused killer was.

Gordon quietly scanned the location, watching as the crews on this mid-May day. In a few minutes, actors would reenact the afternoon of December 4, 1980. One woman, Judith Hayes of Chicora, provided her white 1980 Mercury Cougar to use for the shoot. A Pittsburgh actor, Rick Applegate, was playing the Chief. Another actor, Michael Twaine, played Webb. Gordon Mainhart and State Police Corporal Danny McKnight were on hand to provide technical advice: the location of the cruiser, the location of Webb's car, where the Chief was found.

The producers of the popular Fox show first approached the town a couple of weeks earlier about doing the segment and reenactment after McKnight reached out to them. Mayor Cooper, was initially a bit hesitant. Another crime show, *Unsolved Mysteries* on NBC, had planned to do a similar segment two months earlier but backed out, saying they would do it in the fall instead, and he wasn't sure if doing the show now, with another network, was a conflict. To Cooper and McKnight, though, it didn't matter who did the show. What mattered was getting the word out: the guy who killed the Saxonburg Police Chief was still at large.

The theories about what happened to Donald Webb ranged from the plausible to the absurd. Some people speculated the Providence mob killed him because the murder brought too much attention on their business. Others believed Webb fled the country and was living on a resort island. Some were convinced he was in witness protection after turning on the mob. Still others believed someone was hiding Webb.

McKnight, like other Pennsylvania State Police investigators before him, suspected Webb was in Massachusetts, and hoped the national exposure from the television show would convince someone to come forward.

As he watched from the sidelines on the day of the shoot, Gordon Mainhart was prepared to watch the reenactment. Or so he thought. Seeing the actors play out Greg Adams' death would stir painful memories but nothing, he knew, could be as painful as that afternoon in the ambulance with the Chief in 1980. If it weren't for the police uniform, Gordon wouldn't have recognized his colleague that day. Gordon had seen a lot over the years and considered himself strong. He was in the U.S. Marines for six years, serving in the military police in Vietnam helping refugees as the war neared an end.

As a police officer in Saxonburg, he responded domestics and burglaries and to the fatal crashes where the victims could easily be someone he knew. He had learned how to maintain an emotional barrier on the job while still remaining compassionate. It wasn't always easy. The death of Greg Adams shook everyone in Saxonburg, including him. It touched the heart of the community. It was personal.

On the day of the reenactment, Gordon watched as the crew recorded the police cruiser swing into the parking lot. He watched as the actor portraying Greg Adams walked to the white Mercury Cougar. He knew what would happen next.

The actor playing Greg is knocked to the ground. He is shot. He is beaten and pistol-whipped. Gordon looked at the actor but, in his mind's eye, didn't see a television reenactment. What he saw in that instant were Greg's last moments.

Gordon turned and walked away. He didn't need to keep watching. He knew what would happen next.

Less than a week later, the Mayor, Corporal McKnight and Chief Mainhart were in the show's Washington, D.C. studios to help man the tip lines after the program aired. Danny McKnight and Gordon Mainhart prayed one of the roughly 135 calls that came in would lead them to the killer's location. Some prayers go unanswered, they knew. Hopefully, this would be different.

After the show aired, two letters came into the *America's Most Wanted* offices after the television program aired, one in January of 1990 and the second in February of 1990. Both were addressed to the FBI. Both were signed Donald Webb.

The letter writer expressed regret for killing Chief Gregory Adams. There was a suggestion he might surrender.

Could the killer have a conscience? Could it be this simple? Was this letter authentic? Investigators stifled their optimism.

Ask any detective, and he or she will tell you a story of that believable tip everyone hoped would break the case but, instead, turned out to be false. Sometimes it is an honest mistake: someone overhears a conversation and misinterprets what was said or views a series of events wrong. Sometimes the tip is a cruel hoax.

The letter, believed mailed out of New York, was sent to the FBI lab for analysis. There, the handwriting was examined. The finding: it was unlikely the author of the letter was Webb.

Chapter 6
Moving On

Time does not heal all. It is not a great equalizer. It does not, as a German proverb claims, bring roses. Nor is it the best medicine for anger. It stretches out like a yawning cat, reaching simultaneously forward and back. The mourning creeps into dreams, into those life moments of family where the heart feels the empty space where the dead should be. The resiliency of the human soul overcomes the sorrow to survive. Flowers grow in the soil of grief. The beauty of life blooms eternal. That is what those touched by the life of Chief Adams found as the years passed.

By 2005, Chief Adams had been dead for 25 years. His wife had remarried in 1989. His two sons were now grown. They all had long moved out of Saxonburg.

Most of the original investigators had retired or moved up in the ranks and onto other cases but someone new was always picking at the painful scab of the murder between newer investigations, leaving an unhealed wound.

What was left to follow were informational crumbs, bits in a starving investigation that, in a different time, that might have fallen to the wayside. There was the time someone used Donald Webb's Social Security number in the Midwest, sending investigators scrambling to find the man. It was a case of identity theft. There was an FBI employee in the Midwest with the same name.

The alleged sightings of Webb sipping cocktails on an island. The report he was dead in a Caribbean morgue. Just like the Boston mobster James "Whitey" Bulger, who fled Massachusetts in 1994 after being indicted for nineteen murders and eluded capture for nearly two decades, Donald Webb became the fugitive holy grail for federal agents and state police.

In Saxonburg, the name Gregory Adams was spoken softly, in reverent tones, the pain of the killing reverberating in the decades that followed. A young chief and a chance, fatal encounter. A life defined in history by death. A life unfulfilled. John C. Rhyshek, who was five when the Chief was killed and later became a police chief in Alaska, visits Adams' grave whenever he returns to his hometown. He leaves small mementos to show the Chief is not forgotten. On his desk in Alaska, he keeps a 1979 photo on his desk clipped from the local Pennsylvania newspaper, *The Butler Eagle.*

In it, Rhyshek is standing next to Chief Adams' at a police community safety event. It is a daily reminder of the perils of police work, a life cut and an upended community. "How could something this devastating, this life-changing happen in small-town America, where people make deals by shaking hands, where people still wave?" he asked years later.

Saxonburg physically changed little over the years after the murder. The white clapboard church at the end of Main Street still stood. The Hotel Saxonburg still served up the best food. The volunteer fire department still responded to calls. The police officers still walked along downtown. People still smiled at each other. The hominess of the community, its tightness, its sense of "we are in this together" before it became a national crisis slogan never wavered. But there was that undercurrent of grief, threatening to drown a community buoyed by camaraderie. It was always under the surface. Waiting to rise.

The killing of Chief Adams haunted the town for both its randomness and its lack of conclusion. "It was never a story that went away," said Melinda Berzonski, whose mother, Maria, later owned a downtown coffee and ice cream shop in town.

Beau Sneddon, who as a child played with the Chief's sons and later grew up to become a police officer, said the murder hung over the town "like a dark cloud." His brother, Jeff, born after the slaying, agreed. "There was a presence you could feel."

As the days turned to weeks and the weeks to months and the months to years and years to decades, a hesitant acceptance settled on the community that the killer would never be found. Some believed a fellow mobster killed him. Others thought he had been fatally wounded by the Chief, his body hidden somewhere along the East Coast. Others wondered if he died of natural causes, perhaps under an assumed name. Too much time passed. Too many investigators in too many states came up empty. Hopes of finding the killer was raised, and dashed, too many times.

It also appeared over time Lillian Webb moved on. Investigators discovered she was spending time with a retired and respected Massachusetts defense attorney and the two were seen going to lunch or dinner together. On January 10, 2005, 44 years after marrying Donald, she hired a different attorney and filed for divorce, citing desertion. The name of her divorce attorney highlighted the intersecting lives in a small city.

Former Bristol County District Attorney Ronald A. Pina, who served as the county prosecutor from 1979 to 1991 and was now in private practice, represented her in court. He was in office in those first, intense months when investigators were searching for Webb in New Bedford. (At the time, he was involved in other, headline-grabbing local cases.) The city was small, both in size and interactions.

People traveled in different social circles but there was always that one or two degree of separation in friends, family or neighborhood. As District Attorney, Ronald Pina spent time with lawyers, lawmakers, governors, mayors and business leaders—the core of politics in communities large and small. He also once lived not far from Lillian's New Bedford house.

In the standard fill-in-the-blanks divorce paperwork, Lillian claimed Donald deserted her on or about February of 1980.

She listed her address as Dartmouth. His address was listed as "Parts Unknown." She did not seek a division of property or alimony in her filing. Legal notices of the divorce filing were printed in the local newspaper, *The Standard-Times of New Bedford*, ordering Donald Webb to contact the court by April 19, 2005, on the matter. He never did.

Probate and Family Court Judge Armand Fernandes, Jr. granted the divorce on June 17, 2005, on the grounds of desertion. It took effect September 16, 2005. The decree noted that she could now use her maiden name.

As people moved on with their lives and careers, Saxonburg Police Chief Gordon Mainhart worried the search for Chief Adams' killer was now a low priority for federal investigators. The message he received in March of 2007 seemed to confirm that—and he was angry.

After 26 years on the FBI's "Ten Most Wanted Fugitives" list, Donald Eugene Webb's name was being removed as of March 31, 2007. The case wasn't really closed, Gordon was assured, but the accused killer just didn't meet the criteria to stay on the list. To be on the list, the FBI looked at whether the person had a long criminal record, was still a danger to society and if being on the list would generate the publicity needed to catch him or her. By 2007, Webb was on the FBI fugitive list for 26 years, the longest of any person. There had been some leads over that time but none, not even those generated by television shows, appeared to be valid. Some people now were leaning towards Webb being dead.

The idea for FBI's "Ten Most Wanted Fugitives" list started in 1949 after James Donovan, a reporter from the wire service International News Service (later called United Press International), asked for the names of the people the agency most wanted to catch. The reporter's front-page story in the Washington Daily News garnered so much publicity, the agency decided to formalize the list on March 14, 1950. The first person on that list was a man named Thomas James Holden, accused of gunning down his wife and two brothers-in-law with a .38 during a drunken family argument in Illinois, 18 months after he was paroled from Alcatraz in 1947. Holden, who once escaped from Leavenworth, was caught in Beaverton, Oregon after his mug shot ran on page seven of the Oregonian newspaper June 20, 1950, above ads for Sears and Arthur Murray Dance Studios. Days later, he was caught after an acquaintance turned him in.

The FBI list was considered a success over the years, with many fugitives caught quickly thanks to media publicity. The FBI reports that about 60 percent of those on the list are caught within a year and more than half of those within a month. Most of those on the list who were found far from where the crime occurred, with more than 40 percent outside the United States. For example, between 1998 and 2009, 12 were found in Mexico, four in South America, four in the Middle East, two in the Caribbean, two in Asia and one in Europe and one in Canada.

The Most Wanted list is a way to enhance publicity about fugitives in a community, not as a replacement for law enforcement work. In the beginning, about a third of the cases were solved due to what the FBI called "citizen cooperation."

Nearly 40 percent of fugitives were caught between 1989 and 2009 thanks to publicity. Thanks to social media and the internet, those numbers are expected to keep increasing. The FBI now has a "Wanted" mobile app and actively uses social media to publicize cases.

Earlier, television shows, such as America's Most Wanted, which featured the hunt for Chief Adams' killer, helped catch a number of fugitives. For example, between 1989 and 2009, ten fugitives were caught thanks to tips to the America's Most Wanted show and two were caught thanks to the show *Unsolved Mysteries*, before that network show was canceled, the FBI reported.

However, not all dangerous career criminal fugitives make the FBI list and not everyone stays on it. There is a multistep process to be followed when making the decision of who goes on and who goes off. To get on, first, the FBI's Criminal Investigative Division asks the 56 field officers to submit the names of who they believe should be on the list. Then, the Criminal Investigative Division and the FBI's Office of Public Affairs review the names and come up with suggestions. FBI executive management then makes the final decision.

There are two ways someone is removed from the list. If they are dead, captured or surrender they will be taken off, making way for a new fugitive. The second way is if they no longer fit the criteria to be on the list. Sometimes it is investigators believe, but can't confirm, the fugitive is dead or the person is no longer considered dangerous. By 2007, Donald Webb would be turning 79 years old. Did this mean the FBI thought he was dead or infirm?

Gordon and Corporal Danny McKnight didn't know if Webb was still alive. They didn't know if he was incapacitated. What they wanted were answers. Where had he been all these years? Did anyone help him? How did he escape? What was he doing in Saxonburg? Why did he kill the Chief?

They felt as strongly as they did decades earlier that Webb should be on the FBI's list and appealed to the FBI to keep him there. If a person could kill a cop, he or she should be considered the most dangerous of fugitives. This person would kill again to avoid capture. This person fit the criteria to stay as a Most Wanted fugitive. Their arguments failed to convince the agency. They hoped the decision didn't mean the search for Webb was over. They weren't sure what more they could do to keep it going.

In Massachusetts, as the years passed, what was once a fervent search for Donald Webb became an occasional effort, squeezed between pressing day-to-day assignments. The Massachusetts state trooper tasked with finding fugitives in the Greater New Bedford area in 1982, a man named Jose Gonsalves, often worked with a colleague on the Fall River Department, Detective Preston Paull, who did the same job for his department. Paull was familiar with that loose group with the unimaginative name "Fall River Gang," and kept hoping someone would finally slip up and give up Webb. Secrets, after all, are rarely kept this long. Paull admitted he sometimes obsessed about the case.

He once grabbed Lillian Webb's curbside trash in New Bedford and brought it home. In his garage, he sifted through the food wrappings and cans. Was this the type of food a guy would eat? Is this the amount of trash a single person would generate? He laughs remembering his wife shaking her head when she saw the pile of garbage.

She didn't expect he would bring his job home quite that way. Even though he worked in Fall River, Paull found himself following Lillian along the region's highways and through the city streets of New Bedford. He followed her a few times to a local New Bedford diner where she had breakfast. He remembers once chatting with her at the register as she bought and scratched lottery tickets. "Hope you get a winner," he recalled telling her. She didn't.

Other police investigations involving the extended Webb family in Massachusetts touched on the search for the killer. When State Trooper Joseph Costa in the 1980s watched the Westport home of Lillian's son in an unrelated gaming investigation, he half expected to spot Donald Webb going into the house. Once, he thought he did. It was a man matching the killer's description, a "dead ringer" Costa remembers thinking. Police circled the house. It was someone else.

By this time, most investigators were convinced Lillian Webb knew where her husband was hiding. A few even wondered if he was in her home.

But, as the years passed, they needed evidence to back up those gut feelings that Webb was inside Lillian's house if they were to convince a judge to sign a search warrant allowing them entry. They didn't have it. FBI agents staked out the house, sometimes watching from nearby homes. They talked with neighbors about visitors or strange cars at the house.

They showed them photographs of Donald Webb. No one recognized the man in the photograph. One neighbor, Jocelyn

Allen, said she could see into the yard from the upstairs of her New Bedford home and remembers seeing a few cookouts but never anyone matching Webb's description.

While Massachusetts police still kept occasional watch on the New Bedford house, it appeared to be relegated to the rising pile of outstanding fugitive warrants in the state. However, the FBI and Pennsylvania State Police cast a wider net in the country and abroad. Pennsylvania State Trooper Jim Poydence recalled getting tips of six to eight potential sightings of Webb in the 1980s.

In 1984, police checked out a tip that Webb was sighted by a real estate agent in Hazelton in the Lake Harmony area in the Pocono Mountains, a popular resort area in Pennsylvania. There was a series of burglaries there and members of the Fall River gang were identified as possible suspects. One of the suspects matched the description of Donald Webb. However, by the time authorities were notified, the gang had moved on. It appeared Donald Webb was still "working" in the state.

Another time, a man matching Webb's description was confronted walking off a plane. Another time, he was "seen" vacationing at a resort but it turned out to be someone else. In nearly all of the reported sightings, it was always someone else. When Poydence was eventually promoted and others officially took over, his expertise was so trusted, his notes so detailed, that he still fielded calls about the case.

By the early 1990s, the pages of reports generated by law enforcement in Pennsylvania, Massachusetts and elsewhere in the country reached more than 1,000. The case passed through the hands of more than a dozen state and federal investigators at different points. The FBI case file was eventually officially transferred from Pennsylvania to Massachusetts five years after the killing since it was clear Webb's ties were now in New England.

By the time FBI Special Agent Fred Roberson took over there seemed to be little to follow up. He was at least the third FBI agent in Massachusetts to take the case. The New Bedford FBI office closed in 1983 for a time, the agents transferred to Providence more than 45 minutes and a political world away.

But a few years later logistics and case loads necessitated the need for a Southeastern Massachusetts office to reopen, this time in Lakeville, a small town roughly 20 minutes north of New Bedford where Roberson now worked.

While the search for Chief Adams' killer was one of several cases agents were working on, it was the one Roberson considered the most important. He was aware of what already had been done. If he had questions, he called George Bates and Jack McGraw, who for years doggedly pursued the case for the FBI. He did what others did before him: he went to Lillian's house, he knocked on her door and stood in the doorway, asking her where her husband was. Once, she let him stand inside the foyer because the open door was letting out the heat. None of the interviews were fruitful. "You can only ask 'what do you know' so many times," Roberson later said.

If getting Lillian to talk was tough, watching her house on Hawthorn Street in New Bedford undetected was near impossible. It was a busy street and the type of neighborhood where parking was at a premium. The neighbors were also vigilant. Several times a New Bedford cruiser would roll up on the FBI surveillance team after getting a call about a suspicious vehicle. It became clear quickly: if neighbors could see them, so could Lillian. So, in the mid-1990s, Roberson used what was then a high-tech route to catch the fugitive.

FBI technicians installed a video camera on a pole near the house and at least once a week someone climb up to retrieve the tape. Fred Roberson would then settle into his Lakeville office to watch it in real time. Sometimes he could fast forward. Most of the time he stared at the television screen, looking for a sign of the fugitive. He would watch Lillian drive up to her house in a Cadillac. The garage door would open. As she drove in, he could see the door begin to close inches after the car cleared the garage entrance.

Nobody does that, he remembers thinking. Not unless they are hiding something.

He watched, week after week. The car went in, the door went down. The door went up, the car went out. He saw Lillian behind the wheel. He never saw Donald Webb.

In 1997, Lillian moved to a suburban neighborhood in Dartmouth, the coastal town bordering New Bedford to the west. Surveillance on the house wasn't as intense but Lillian still appeared to be cautious. Even in retirement, Preston Paull, the Fall River cop, found himself still driving by her house. She was always wary, he said, never letting her guard down.

By the mid 2000s, the average person in New Bedford and the surrounding communities knew little of Donald Webb, even though he was part of local lore in the circle of older, retired law enforcement officers.

Some cops, either children at the time of the killing or born years later, knew nothing about the killer possibly in their midst or the slaying of Police Chief Gregory Adams in a small community in Pennsylvania. But for those who had been on the job in the early 1980s, particularly on the Massachusetts State Police and FBI, it was a case still open, unfinished business, where stories about Lillian and Donald morphed into lore. There was the tale about a Vermont state trooper spotted Lillian pulled along the side of the highway. He stopped. Webb wasn't in the car but some speculated he was relieving himself in the woods.

The tale about Lillian making a U-turn on the highway when she spotted a trooper behind her. Or the times the accused killer was in Canada but no one could find him. The stories were embellished with time and retelling, until reality blurred with fantasy. There was always one constant though. Lillian Webb. Those close to the case were convinced she knew where the killer was. How could they prove it?

For law enforcement, it was always a cat and mouse game where no one ever saw the mouse.

Chapter 7
New Look

Phil Torsney first spotted the photo of the cop killer on the wall at the FBI Academy in Quantico in 1984. At the time, it had been four years since Chief Gregory Adams was shot to death and the Saxonburg killer was still on the FBI's Top Ten Most Wanted list. Torsney was fresh out of the academy at the time and remembers thinking, "I'd like to catch that guy."

Catching people is what Torsney did for most of his career in the FBI. He worked in Atlanta for two years then spent most of his career in Cleveland, where he investigated everything from bank robberies to drug trafficking rings. But his real talent was finding fugitives and he picked up an odd but useful skill in the field along the way.

"You ever been arrested?" he would ask a guy who was stopped. Then he would run a criminal history on the suspect—and ask for the National Crime Information Center (NCIC) fingerprint classification of the person's prints. He would look at the fingers and mentally compare them with the coding from NCIC—each number in the classification correlating to loops, arches and whorls. The bad guys were always stunned when he did that. It wasn't a foolproof method but it gave him probable cause to bring the suspect in. Plus, he was rarely wrong.

Torsney eventually lead a specialized squad targeting fugitives in the Cleveland area—then he was sent to Boston where he would work with teams of federal and state law enforcement investigators to find one of the most notorious fugitive mobsters: James Joseph "Whitey" Bulger, Jr.

Bulger fled Massachusetts in 1994 after being tipped off by a then-FBI agent that he was about to be indicted by a federal grand jury in connection with nineteen murders. That agent, John Connolly, used the mobster as a confidential informant for years to develop information about the rival Patriarca crime family and largely ignored crimes committed by Bulger's Winter Hill gang.

Connolly, who grew up with Bulger, was later convicted of federal racketeering charges and second-degree murder in Florida in connection with Bulger's crimes. The case tarnished the public image of the FBI and was a cringing embarrassment to the honest agents in the field. Catching Whitey Bulger was a top priority.

Torsney was first pulled into the Bulger case—as were other agents—on a temporary basis in 2000. He tracked leads in Canada and Boston several times after that, even when he returned to Cleveland. Then he got a call in 2009 from the squad supervisor of the Bulger task force, Rich Teahan.

"Come back to Massachusetts."

Torsney was excited when he got the call. He worked with both Teahan and another member of the task force, Bob Patnaude, during his other temporary assignments working the Bulger fugitive case. One of his career goals was to catch a Top Ten Fugitive and this was his chance.

Noreen Gleason, the new Assistant Special Agent for the FBI's criminal division in Boston, was the one who officially tapped Torsney for the revitalized task force. When the New Jersey native arrived in Boston in January of 2008, her boss, Warren Bamford, gave her five priorities. At the top was catching Bulger. There was already a Bulger fugitive task force in place when she got there but the hunt, after so many years, seemed stalled and stagnant.

The other investigators did a good job but she felt the case needed a sharp kick-start. She wanted some new blood. People who worked well with others, who were not from Boston, who weren't territorial in investigations, who knew how to listen to people, who would look at the investigation a bit differently.

Several people she knew and respected in the bureau mentioned Torsney. The second agent she wanted on the team was an agent she once worked with: Tommy MacDonald, who worked out of the New York office in the Violent Crimes Task Force.

MacDonald worked bank robberies and in 2007, when another agent was promoted, took on the 1979 cold case disappearance of six-year-old Etan Patz, who went missing in New York City while walking to school alone for the first time. The disappearance of the child, who was later presumed dead, helped spark the national missing children search movement.

While in New York, Tommy MacDonald hit the case of Etan Patz' disappearance hard. He interviewed witnesses again, reexamined potential suspects and eventually developed a 50-page document the press called the "Patzifesto." (Another agent, Jed Salter, eventually took over the case and in 2012 a former bodega worker was charged in the boy's murder.) Tommy's dedication to cases was noticed and his name was at the top of Gleason's list when it came to bolstering the Bulger team.

She knew Torsney and MacDonald both were kind individuals who could approach and talk with people from all walks of life, never making someone feel inferior. And they listened. They heard what people were saying and how they said it. They could read a situation and an individual well. They also had that uncanny ability to see what might be missing in a case. That was important in finding Bulger. She wanted them full-time on the team.

Phil Torsney and Tommy MacDonald talked by phone about the Bulger case several times before heading to Boston for their new, temporary full-time assignments in 2009.

"I'm not going to sit around on my ass," Phil remembers the younger agent telling him.

"I'm not either," Phil answered.

The two agents brought in by Gleason had few ties to Boston. It was by design. Local law enforcement members—including those on the Massachusetts state police—were leery of working with the FBI after the Bulger-Connolly fiasco. Could they trust the Feds? Should they? Gleason, Torsney and Mac-Donald knew catching Bulger was important—but so was rebuilding bonds with local law enforcement in Massachusetts. The FBI agents brought into Boston were street guys from across the country with no ties to Massachusetts politics, politicians or the former agent who tipped Bulger off. They came in with a clean slate and made sure local law enforcement knew it.

Phil and Tommy worked the Bulger Task Force in Boston for about a year. Occasionally they were sent back to their original assignments in Cleveland and New York when cases there needed their attention. Once, Phil was called back to Cleveland to work a serial killing case after 11 bodies were found buried in a back yard of a man named Anthony Sowell. While trying to find Bulger, though, Phil would often mention the name of another fugitive to Tommy: a guy by the name of Donald Eugene Webb who killed a Pennsylvania police chief in 1980. "The guy murdered a police chief. He needs to be caught," Phil repeatedly told him. "He can't get away with that."

Bulger, though, was the immediate focus, not a decades-old murder in Pennsylvania, and the agents tried to look at the case through a different investigative lens. What if they were looking for the wrong person? Maybe they should focus on his longtime girlfriend, Catherine Greig, instead. They spent years circulating Whitey Bulger's photo and tracking down possible sightings, each time coming up short. Whitey was now an old, bald guy—so nondescript, his doppelgangers were at grocery stores, gas stations and coffee shops across Canada and the United States. He looked like someone's grandpa, tooling around in a Buick in the slow speed lane on the highway.

Noreen Gleason knew Bulger was a dangerous man and wouldn't think twice about killing a woman. If they treated his girlfriend as a missing person, a woman in danger, would that make it easier to find him? What if she was dead? Was she one of the more than 40,000 unidentified dead in the country? How would they know? Catherine Greig had never been fingerprinted. They didn't even have good photos of her. Focusing on Greig as a possible Bulger victim could finally lead to the mobster. They knew Greig had breast implants and plastic surgery before fleeing with Bulger in 1994 so Phil and Tommy, working with FBI analyst Roberta "Bobbi" Hastings, located her doctors and, through court orders, obtained the serial number for the implants to compare, if needed, with any on unidentified bodies. They also eventually hit the jackpot with the plastic surgery files. There, Tommy found newer photographs of Greig taken by doctors, never before seen by investigators.

Tommy was already back in New York, working another case, when the FBI released the photos of Greig to the news media in 2011. And the calls quickly came in. Soon, they had information that Bulger and Greig were in California and on June 22, 2011, the Los Angeles FBI Fugitive Task Force at an apartment house in Santa Monica arrested the pair. Bulger, then 81, was using the alias Charlie Gasko. Greig was posing as his wife, Carol.

Phil flew out from Boston the next day on a commercial flight with squad supervisor Rich Teahan and a U.S. Marshal named Neil Sullivan the next day and returned on the FBI director's jet with Bulger and Greig to Massachusetts.

The flight back to Boston was joyous. The Moby Dick of fugitives was in handcuffs. When they landed at Logan Airport, Phil's bosses—Noreen Gleason and John Foley, both Assistant Special Agents in charge—met the plane to congratulate the agents.

"You know what the next one is, right? Next is Donald Eugene Webb," Phil told Noreen Gleason. "We have to start working on that."

Phil was set to turn 57 in less than two years, the mandatory retirement age. He figured he would have to work fast to catch Webb.

He did counter-terrorism work in Afghanistan soon after Bulger was caught but once back, started looking through the

FBI Webb case files. There were thousands of pages in more than nineteen volumes. He compiled a list of people to talk with. He tried to figure out where Webb would go for help, what family members would help. It was clear from the files Webb's ties to blood relatives were frayed.

His parents were dead. So was his brother in California. Another distant relative hadn't seen Webb in decades. A few cousins in Oklahoma years earlier, apparently unaware Webb was a fugitive, had turned to their local newspaper, the Oklahoman, to help track down their long lost relative. Phil drove down to Dartmouth to get a look at Lillian Webb's house. She was now Webb's only family. If anyone knew where Webb was, she would, Phil suspected. He teamed up with other investigators, including Massachusetts State Trooper Curtis Cinelli who he worked with on the Bulger case, to interview some old time crooks.

He began developing some investigative theories. There was a strong chance Webb was dead, Phil knew. There had been one tip to America's Most Wanted that Webb died shortly after the murder and his body was dumped in a river by one of his "buddies."

Phil checked the National Missing and Unidentified Persons System– commonly called NamUs – for unclaimed bodies matching Webb's description, paying close attention to bodies found in rivers, but came up with nothing.

Webb could also have just gone off the grid, assumed a new identity like Bulger did, and was living a new life in retirement—or simply died of old age.

Phil's own retirement clock was ticking and, as the 2013 date neared, he knew there was a good chance he wouldn't find Webb. So, he did the next best thing: he convinced his colleague, Tommy MacDonald, to pick up the case.

Tommy was back in New York when Bulger was finally caught but he had stayed in close contact with Phil as that investigation neared a close. His colleague had mentioned the Pennsylvania murder several times before but Tommy had been focused on the Bulger hunt. Plus, what more could he do that so many others hadn't been able to do before him?

It took a few phone calls from Phil to pull Tommy in. The guy killed a police chief, Phil kept telling him. He can't get away with it. It would be a challenging case to pick up, Tommy MacDonald knew, and he liked a challenge. Cold cases can be solved if you hit the right door at the right time. Maybe this was the right time.

There were some logistical and administrative issues Tommy needed to address first before he took on the case. By 2015, Tommy had been transferred to the FBI office in Portland, Maine and the case was officially in the FBI Lakeville, Massachusetts office—a small town not far from New Bedford, Massachusetts (the FBI New Bedford office had been closed years earlier and the agents relocated, first to Providence, Rhode Island then eventually to Lakeville). Both Lakeville and Portland, however, were under the FBI Boston Division Office. When he learned no one was actively working on what was now a cold case, he asked his boss in Boston if he could take it on. Go for it, he was told.

First, he talked with one of the agents in the Lakeville office, Don Kornek. He knew Kornek from his days in New York. Kornek had experience talking with organized crime wise guys and their families. Tommy considered this the first good sign for the case. They could hit the streets to talk with the old-time mobsters, some now in nursing homes. He also enlisted the help of another agent, Richard Pires, whose expertise in building a rapport with people in interviews and investigations was valuable.

Second, he read the FBI case file and tried to see what he could do in 2015. It appeared all the investigative I's had been dotted, all the T's crossed, he saw. He called the Pennsylvania state police to see about reviewing their files. Maybe there was a way to use what they already knew to get someone to talk, he thought.

Third, Tommy looked at what physical evidence could be re-tested thanks to advances in forensic technology. Evidence from both the cruiser and the getaway car was preserved.

Could they retest it for DNA and enter it into a database?

Then, they would publicize the case again. The FBI sent out press releases to media across the country, with extra attention to Pennsylvania, Florida, Rhode Island and Massachusetts, announcing a $100,000 reward for information leading to where Webb was.

It was a long shot but one worth taking.

There were a few problems from the start, however. Many of Webb's "criminal associates" were dead or so infirm they couldn't remember where they were. Those who were still alive and lucid were as uncooperative as they were decades earlier.

Tommy met with one former member of the Fall River gang who was locked up in Rhode Island. The meeting lasted about ten minutes. Tommy did most of the talking. When the guy, now elderly with an oxygen tank at his side, heard what the agent wanted, he had a simple answer. It was an expletive followed by "I'll never cooperate with you guys." Then the con walked out.

Another Fall River crew member imprisoned in Massachusetts was a bit more pleasant and talkative. But what he had to say wasn't that helpful.

A jewel thief in the Midwest who knew associates of Webb was interviewed by retired FBI Agent Dick Wrenn. Stricken with Parkinson's, the thief could recall little.

Tommy turned his focus on Frank Lach, one of Webb's close associates who went to prison rather than cooperate with a federal grand jury trying to get information on Webb's whereabouts. Phil Torsney earlier had gone to Florida, where Lach was living in a house, to try to talk with the Rhode Island man. Lach was polite but wouldn't talk. Tommy and fellow agent Richard Pires tried an indirect approach to see what Lach might know by interviewing people on the outer circles of his life. He talked with Lach's ex-wife. He talked with the girlfriend of a Chicago mobster who drove to Florida occasionally with Lach's sister. They talked with a guy convicted of murder and some other people.

Eventually, in February of 2016, the two agents decided to

pay Lach a visit in Florida.

The once burly Lach, who loved to tip high and dress sharp, was now living in an assisted living/nursing home called Avalon next to Interstate 95 with the constant hum of 18-wheelers in the background. He was living in a single room with cinderblock walls and a single, small window, sharing a bathroom with a woman who suffered from dementia. He was suffering from COPD and was undergoing dialysis several times a week. The man who loved to socialize had few regular visitors, except for his sister who would travel from Rhode Island to see him. He was a shell, physically, of the old gangster.

When Tommy and Rich walked into his room, telling him they came all the way to Florida just to talk with him, Lach was dismissive.

"I don't know why you guys are here," Rich recalled him telling the agents. "I'm going to tell you the same thing I told the others. Nothing."

That day the agents spent more than an hour talking with the old man, trying to get him to say something about Webb. Lach seemed to enjoy the company.

"I have to tell you, I was going to tell you guys to fuck off when you came in," Rich recalled Lach saying.

The next day the agents were back. Furniture was sparse in the room that was half the size of a motel room. A bed shoved in a corner. A bureau. A television. A walker with yellow tennis balls tucked on the bottom. A chair. A portable potty. They spent three hours with Lach, shifting seats between the chair and potty-chair. Sometimes a nurse came in to conduct a medical procedure or test. Sometimes Lach would doze off. Occasionally the woman who lived in the adjoining room would wander in and Tommy or Rich would lead her back to her own quarters.

When the agents left Florida, they felt they made a connection with Lach even if he refused to say where Webb was.

One thing also stuck out. "Why are you digging this up?" Lach had asked Pires. "It's all ancient history. Just leave it alone."

But there was something in how Lach talked, the language he used, which intrigued the agents. Lach kept using the past tense when talking about Webb.

What if Webb was dead, what if he died of natural causes?

A month later, the federal agents returned to Florida to talk with Lach.

They spent hours on the first day of the return visit, chatting generally, trying to get some specifics about Webb while encouraging him to eat the food brought to the room by the staff. Lach wouldn't budge.

When they returned the next day, Rich Pires brought a box of cannoli, an immunity letter from the Butler County prosecutor's office—and $10,000 in cash. He placed all three before Lach. The $10,000 could be a tenth of the $100,000 reward Lach could get if he told where Webb was.

Lach looked at the money.

One hundred thousand dollars would get you a nice place to live out your life, the agents told him.

"You know, I won't lie, the money would be nice because I would like to tip some of the ladies here who were so nice," Rich recalled Lach saying.

As the hours stretched out in the room, Tommy kept pressing him to do the right thing, to put the case to rest, to tell them where Donald Webb was. Unburden your soul.

Lach seemed to soften, his voice introspective. "If I betray my oath, my whole life was meaningless," he told them, the agents recalled.

He didn't talk about what he knew about Webb when called before a federal grand jury and, eventually, did seven years in federal prison. Why talk now? he asked them.

As day turned to night, the conversation continued. It was after dinner was served, hours after the agents arrived, when Lach made an admission.

"He's dead."

He told them a Providence area funeral home with mob connections handled the funeral sometime in the 1990s. The body was either cremated or buried under a fake name. He didn't name the funeral home. He did give them the fake name used. "He was sure he was dead," Rich recalled. "His demeanor changed. It was almost like a weight had been lifted off his shoulders."

When the agents returned for a third day, Lach appeared to regret what he had told them. "He was trying to back-pedal," Rich said. "Tommy and I saw that as he regretted what he told us."

Once back in New England, investigators looked at which funeral directors would likely handle burials of people who were using assumed names. There were some funeral homes in Rhode Island, frequented by organized crime members, rumored to have handled those types of services over the years.

However, those funeral directors had either died or the businesses had closed. There were no records of burials under the name provided by Lach (and the man with that name was very much alive). There were no death certificates either. Donald Webb may have been dead but there was no record of it.

When Tommy decided to take on the case, one of his first calls in 2015 was to the Pennsylvania State Police investigative unit. He detected hesitancy on the other end when he talked with Pennsylvania State Police Trooper Chris Birckbichler, who was now in charge of the state police criminal investigative unit, including cold cases.

At the top of Birckbichler's list for years was the slaying of Chief Greg Adams. He grew up in the shadow of the case. He was just a kid, 14 years old, driving home from the store with his dad, Dale, a state trooper at the time, when they saw the waves of state police moving into the Saxonburg area. He watched as his dad pulled up to a cruiser, driver window to driver window cop-style, to find out from Trooper Ron Conrad, what happened.

He listened as they talked about the death of the Saxonburg Police Chief and the manhunt for the killer. His dad dropped him off at home ten miles away, told him to tell his mother to lock the doors and stay inside then left for Saxonburg to join the search. When Chris later joined the state police in 2000, after serving in the Navy, he eventually was assigned to the Butler barracks criminal investigative unit five years later. He was filling the slot vacated by Trooper Mark Bardzil, who was promoted and would be transferred, standard procedure when promotions were made. He was also taking over that trooper's cases. One was a cold case. It was the search for Saxonburg Police Chief Gregory Adams' killer.

He called his dad that day.

"I have Greg Adams' case," he remembers telling him.

"Greg was my friend," his father, now retired, answered. "I worked with Greg. Do your best on the case."

"I will do the best I can," Chris told his father.

Chris pulled out the eight binders of reports on the case at the barracks and started to read, juggling that research with current homicides and other investigations. In the following months and years, he looked through national databases and talked with now-retired investigators.

He quickly discovered there was little in Pennsylvania left to check on. What he did hear were quirky stories about the case and the search, some with questions still unanswered. One story was that the FBI screwed up, that Webb was found on a Caribbean island vacationing but slipped away. There was another that Webb was in a witness protection program. The stories lingered for years in local law enforcement gossip. Now, years later, with a FBI agent on the line saying he was looking for help finding the killer, Chris was leery. Could he trust this person?

"I have a couple of questions first," Birckbichler told the agent.

He asked about the stories of missed chances, of the Caribbean island, of the possibility Webb was being protected.

"Let me find out and get back to you," the agent answered. Days later, the phone in Chris Birckbichler's state police office rang. Tommy MacDonald had the answers. There was no screw up. Webb wasn't on that island. There had been a dead guy there who someone claimed looked like Webb. It wasn't the fugitive. The FBI checked. Also, Webb wasn't in witness protection. At that moment, the Pennsylvania state trooper who grew up in the shadow of the hunt felt there was a good chance the case would finally be resolved.

Tommy MacDonald liked to make to-do lists. If he completed eight out of ten items, it was a pretty good day. He preferred, of course, to finish ten. So, when he decided to find the man who killed Chief Adams, the first thing he did was write on a file folder what he needed to do.

One: Review all the files. Two: Talk with the retired investigators who knew the nuances of what was in those files. Three: Talk with people close to the killer.

But before he could dig deep into the case, he needed to take one basic step to show he was serious. He needed to go to Saxonburg where it all started. He needed to talk, face to face, with Birckbichler. Showing up would send the message he was determined to see the case through.

He drove to FBI office in Pittsburgh on July 6, 2015 to talk with agents in the office, then to Butler to meet with Birckbichler, learn what he could about the murder and view the crime scenes. At the Butler barracks, one of the first troopers he met was a young man who grew up in Saxonburg. It highlighted to him how the death of Chief Adams, and the killer's escape, still hung dark over the community.

Tommy and Chris Birckbichler hit it off right away. The two were focused, bright and social. Tommy was forthright about what he had so far: he still didn't know where Donald Eugene Webb was. But he was firm about what he hoped to accomplish: finding the killer dead or alive.

The first step for Tommy was seeing where it all started. They drove by the Saxonburg police station to the Agway store and looked at the area where the Chief fought for his life behind the nearby house. They drove to the spot where his gun was found. He later met with one of the last people to see the Chief before he was killed—the former the administrative assistant, Sue Haggerty, who was now a judge. She gave him a list of long-retired investigators who worked the case and people in town who knew the Chief.

Later, he would call a long list of retired Pennsylvania state troopers and FBI agents, sometimes asking for suggestions or to provide personal impressions typed reports couldn't capture. He was laying a firm foundation to carefully and methodically build on.

Jim Poydence was expecting the call from Tommy inquiring about the case. Jim's close friend and former FBI agent, Pete McCann, gave him a heads up that a new agent in New England was taking a new—and hard—look at finding Donald Webb.

Over the years, even in retirement, Jim and Pete would field calls about the case and would offer whatever insight they could. Their memories were sharp – and Jim still had copies of his notes on the case. Since 1980, the case had changed hands many times both on the state and federal side and, each time, investigators would seek out those who were there from the start.

The first thing Jim noticed was the intensity of the FBI agent. The agent wanted to know who might be the best people to interview, what were his impressions of people. It was the first of many phone calls between the two. He hoped this renewed interest would finally lead to an answer.

Before leaving Pennsylvania, Tommy MacDonald had one more stop to make. One of the now-elderly former criminal associates of the killer told investigators there was a story circulating that Webb never made it out of the state alive after the murder. A critically injured Webb, suffering a gunshot wound, had gone to a hotel where some of his cohorts hung out in Carbon County, Pennsylvania after the shooting and died. There was a cemetery behind the place and, the way the story went, Webb's buddies noticed a grave had been dug for a funeral the next day. They dumped the body in the grave, covered it up and waited for an unsuspecting family to later lower a casket over it. A double funeral, of sorts.

Tommy had shared that story with his former partner, Phil Torsney, after the two ran the Market Square 10K in Portsmouth, New Hampshire. It could be true, Phil told him. The mob back then did things like that. It was worth checking out.

So, after spending a few days in Butler and Saxonburg, Tommy drove four and a half hours to the historic northeastern Pennsylvania town of Jim Thorpe in the Lehigh Gorge roughly 270 miles away. There he checked out the spot where Webb was rumored to have spent his last hours.

Lantern Lodge and Macaluso's restaurant were established businesses, well known to tourists and residents. Those were also the places some of Webb's associates favored in the 1970s and 80s. The first thing Tommy MacDonald noted when he pulled up to the businesses was the cemetery nearby, up on a hill. And he could see an open grave.

Could the story be true?

For three days, MacDonald checked burial records at three cemeteries and two FBI agents from Philadelphia assigned to the Evidence Response Team, a specialized evidence collection unit, did a site survey for possible burial sites. Were any graves dug in the days after the Saxonburg Chief was killed? Was anyone buried?

They could find nothing to corroborate the tale.

Another dead end.

Tommy returned to New England and spent most of the summer of 2015 reading the Pennsylvania State police investigative files on the death of Chief Adams. The administrative manager in Chris Birckbichler's office by the name of Patty Ice, and the women she supervised, spent hours scanning the files onto a disc for the agent. Reading page after page brought him to that December 4, 1980, afternoon and the months that followed.

The reports were detailed. The shoe-leather put into the case to identify the killer was fascinating reading. After viewing the crime scenes, he could now put the reports in perspective. He could see in his minds-eye where those investigators had gone, what they had done, what obstacles they faced and all they accomplished against the odds. He needed to take the next step and bring it to an end. He was convinced the killer's wife could help do it.

In the months that followed, Tommy stopped by Lillian's house in Dartmouth. The visits were curt but cordial. He could tell she clearly didn't enjoy seeing him at the door.

The FBI had increased the reward for Webb's capture to $100,000 as 2015 came to a close. The reward was announced on the anniversary of the Chief's murder.

The thought behind the reward was simple: was if morality couldn't convince someone to come forward, maybe greed could. But money hadn't worked when a $50,000 reward initially was offered and the higher figure hadn't convinced one of Webb's closest associates, Frank Lach, to talk.

Tommy thought back again to the Bulger case and what had worked then. Could they try something similar?

He knew it often was best not to let the families of murder victims know the intricacies of an investigation. That was particularly true in old cases. Raising hope prematurely could be cruel to those living with unresolved loss. Moving forward carefully and thoughtfully was necessary before approaching a family. He also knew it was important, as a case heated, to let the family know what was going on. He didn't want Chief Gregory Adams' family to learn about movement in the investigation through news reports.

This was a delicate balance: protecting a family against false hope and giving them as much information as possible. Before Tommy spoke with Chief Gregory Adams' family, he wanted to make sure he had a plan on how to handle the case. Photos helped break the Bulger case and he wondered if there was some way it could also help find Webb.

Maybe showing the killer's wife some photos of the Adams family would appeal to her sense of empathy. Maybe it would finally bring home to her how much the family needed an answer.

Tommy called Mary Ann to tell her about the increased reward and asked if she had any photos he could use. The pictures would be used both to publicize the reward and to show Lillian Webb. He hoped showing Lillian the photos would convince her to reveal the whereabouts of her husband.

He then contacted the Pittsburgh FBI office where Special Agent Brian Fox worked. Fox's family owned Fox Funeral Home in Saxonburg not far from where the Chief had been killed and was where Chief Adams' wake had been held. He had a simple request for the Pittsburgh agent: Could you contact the Chief's widow, Mary Ann Jones, who was now remarried, and get some photos?

Mary Ann tried to stay on the sidelines of the criminal investigation over the years. She was pragmatic, sensible and knew if there were a major break in the case, someone would contact her. Life continued just as it had since the late afternoon of December 4, 1980 when her world shattered.

When Agent Fox contacted her in 2015, right after her grandson was born, Mary Ann wasn't sure what good showing family photos would do. But she was willing to give this new plan a shot so she gave the agent a picture of her and her two sons along with a family photo with her grandson. Her expectations were low.

Tommy had already been to Lillian Webb's Dartmouth home once by that time. The first time, in the spring of 2015, Lillian talked with him and fellow agent Don Kornek through the front door for about 50 minutes. She insisted she didn't know where her now ex-husband was. Later, she called to say she didn't need to talk with them again.

The second time, a few months later, they came by with photos of Webb's family the FBI had in the case file. Tommy thought she appeared to enjoy looking at those snapshots. She and Donald Webb had gone out to California once, decades earlier, to visit his family. Clearly, the photos brought back pleasant memories.

Then he pulled out photos of the Chief's family. She appeared annoyed. She insisted, yet again, she didn't know where her husband was.

The Chief's widow wasn't surprised when she learned about the woman's reaction and refusal to talk about the accused killer. She didn't expect, after nearly four decades, a couple of photos would sway her.

Tommy kept going back to the Dartmouth house, though. Over the course of a year and a half, he knocked on Lillian's door at least eight times. Sometimes Lillian Webb would come to the door. Sometimes she wouldn't. When she did open the door, leaving the agents on the front stoop, her answer to the question was always the same. She didn't know where Donald Webb was.

In 1980, Pennsylvania investigators gathered the blood-covered snow where Chief Gregory Adams fought for his life and placed the samples in little tin cups. Back at the lab, the snow was evaporated and the blood tested for type. A few weeks later, on December 21, 1980, when the killer's getaway white Cougar was recovered in Rhode Island, the blood found soaked under the car mat and on the door panel was also recovered and tested.

Investigators knew the Type O belonged to Donald Webb, the Type A to Chief Adams. There was little more testing they could do back then. At the time of the killing, the idea that DNA could be exacted from the blood at a crime scene to positively identify a suspect or that information could be used in court was a law enforcement dream. The concept that there might be a national database for DNA comparison was a fantasy for those on the front lines. But forensic technology and what can be gleaned from evidence changed by 2016 and investigators knew there might be a way to learn if Donald Eugene Webb was dead, his body unclaimed somewhere in the country, or one of the many unidentified suspects known only by the DNA left behind at a crime scene.

Tucked safely away in a large microwave-sized box in one of the three locked evidence rooms at the Butler State Police barracks were the tins, the floor mat and other evidence taken from the Mercury Cougar. The blood in the tins was too old, too disintegrated to extract a useable DNA sample for CODIS entry. But the technicians in the Pennsylvania State Police Bureau of Forensic Sciences laboratory in Greensburg found success with the floor mat and the bloody batting beneath it. They were able to exact a DNA profile from the blood, believed to be that of Donald Webb, and planned to enter it into the FBI's National Combined DNA Indexing System (CODIS) database. It would be yet another "I" dotted in the investigation, one that could help them either identify a dead Webb or track his possible crimes committed after the slaying.

Under CODIS, the DNA profile of the unknown suspect is entered into the system and compared with a national DNA database of those convicted of certain types of crimes or with the DNA taken at crime scenes where the suspect is unknown. If there is a match, or "hit," the agency entering the information is notified. There can be a match with a known offender or a match to another yet unknown suspect. This can help investigators identify suspects or link unknown crimes, such as serial killings.

If there is a match, the laboratory will confirm the results. Names of the suspects or other identifying information are not in the CODIS software. To get that information, investigators must contact the state or agency that entered the profile.

The rules for entering DNA into the CODIS systems are strict and not all samples can be entered. Steps are taken to insure the privacy of those whose DNA has been entered: the samples of convicts are given numerical codes, if there's a hit, the name of the suspect can only be obtained from the law enforcement agency which sent it in.

The DNA profile sample taken from a crime scene where the suspect is unknown is allowed into CODIS. That is because the CODIS system is set up to identify unknown suspects in crimes.

The DNA profile sample taken from a known suspect, such as a sample taken with a swab, is not. That is because the suspect is known.

The DNA profile sample of a victim's blood found at the scene is not. That is because the victim has been identified.

The DNA profile from bloodstains of a suspect taken from his or her own clothing is not. Neither is the DNA from a victim found on the suspect's clothing.

Entering the DNA profile sample from the Mercury Cougar found in Rhode Island shortly after the Chief was killed originally fell under the "not allowed" category. That was because the suspect, Donald Eugene Webb, had been identified and the blood was found in his own vehicle.

But for every rule, there is an exception and Pennsylvania State Police Corporal Chris Birckbichler, with help from members of the State Police Bureau of Forensic Sciences laboratory in Greensburg, found it.

A law enforcement agency could plead its case to the FBI by filing an affidavit, detailing the reasons why the profile should be entered. It took time to get it right, but that is what Chris did.

He laid out the evidence in the case: where blood was found at the scene in Saxonburg and in the car in Rhode Island, how a man was seen limping, how the car found in Rhode Island was seen driving off. He detailed the lengths investigators took to find the suspect, how there were concerns the man might be one of the unidentified dead in the country. The affidavit was similar to the criminal complaint filed in 1980 charging Webb with murder.

Roughly two months after filing the affidavit, the DNA profile entered into the CODIS system in August of 2016. There were no matches.

Entering the DNA into CODIS was just one more item to be checked off in the investigation. There were a few other things left. FBI Special Agent Tommy MacDonald turned back to what worked in the Bulger case: photos. The images the FBI had of Donald Webb were decades old. The digitally age-progressed photos of Webb publically distributed just weren't the same as the real thing. Was there a chance Lillian might have newer photos of her now ex-husband? Was there a chance those pictures were in her home? He was going to see.

Tommy MacDonald focused on the highway as he drove south on Route 24 on November 16, 2016. It was dark and getting late. He was set to be up early the next morning with a team of specialized FBI agents with the Evidence Response Team to search Lillian Webb's house in Dartmouth before five, right around the time she would be leaving to walk her dog. Armed with a federal search warrant, they hoped to find new photos of Donald Webb in the house, along with clues that might lead them to where the fugitive might be. The search warrant, sealed to the public, allowed the agents to take specific items such as photographs of the wanted killer, hopefully ones depicting a post-1980 Webb. If the agents saw more than what was specified on the warrant and wanted it, Lillian would have to agree. It wasn't ideal but it was a first step.

On the ride down, MacDonald called a retired FBI agent, Fred Roberson, to talk about what was coming up the next day and for some last minute suggestions. The two had talked many times about the case even though Roberson retired from the FBI in 1999. That Webb had not been found gnawed at Roberson, just as it had with the other retired FBI and state police investigators who worked the case before him. A young police chief with a young family was dead and a cop killer was free.

The years changed none of that.

MacDonald listened as Roberson offered some suggestions on where to look once they got into the house—and what to look for.

These guys were known to put things in false home sewer drains, Roberson told him. They hid things under floorboards and in curtain rods.

And you might also find hidden rooms or hidden compartments in that house, Roberson said.

Good advice, MacDonald thought. *Very good advice.*

When Tommy MacDonald later spoke with members of the Evidence Response Team, he passed on the information and stressed one point. Be on the lookout for hidden compartments.

The FBI Evidence Response team is a specialized unit comprised of crime scene collection experts, canine search teams, underwater search teams and agents specializing in handling what could be considered hazardous evidence. It is an elite evidence unit skilled in the latest forensic collection methods and tools to deal with complex crime scenes or catastrophic incidents. Sometimes the scenes are like archeological digs, as it was when the remains of a Boston nightclub owner named Steven DiSarro who went missing in 1993 were uncovered behind a Providence mill building in 2016. Sometimes they are horrific attacks, such as the Boston Marathon bombing in 2013 where three people were killed and more than 200 injured.

The FBI pulled up to the 28 Maplecrest Drive in Dartmouth, Massachusetts, shortly before five in the morning as planned on that November day. A stunned Lillian was in her driveway as MacDonald approached her.

"We have a search warrant," MacDonald remembers telling her. "You can leave if you want or you can stay."

Lillian Webb stayed. She went back into the house and sat at the kitchen table as the FBI agents searched the house. In the few times Lillian allowed him inside, Tommy had never been beyond the family room couch. This search warrant opened the house up.

Tommy noticed a large portrait of Webb. It looked like a painting crafted from a photograph. He noted the cross, crafted from the type of palms handed out on Palm Sunday, pinched in the frame.

"Is that Donald?" he asked her, indicating the painting.

"No," she insisted, Tommy recalled. "That is not Donald."

There was another photograph of Donald in the bedroom, narrow cards circulated at wakes tucked onto the side. There was no card for Donald Webb. Tommy would later check the names of the men on those prayer cards to make sure they were not new aliases used by Webb—they weren't.

There were some photographs of Lillian's dogs and the ashes from one of the animals that had died.

The church bulletin from a Fall River Catholic church caught his attention. It listed a Mass for Donald Webb. Did this mean there was a chance the fugitive was dead? If he was, where was the body?

The basement of the home was fully finished and furnished. It could easily be used as an in-law living setup: private and comfortable. It was there, close to two hours into the search, they found a shower stall-sized hidden room in the basement tucked inside a closet stuffed with clothes. The "door" to that hiding place slid across the closet clothing rod and popped open when pressed. Inside was a black "Super Cane" hanging on the wall and three cardboard boxes of silver coins. At the top of the hidden room door was a hook lock, fastened with masking tape. The lock, on the inside of the room, was at the top of the door. Too high for Lillian to reach. Just the right height for someone like Donald Eugene Webb.

"Whose cane is this?" Lillian was asked.

She told the FBI agents she didn't know, MacDonald recalled.

She first said the hidden room was there when she moved in. She told them she didn't know who built it. Later, she said the room was a place she could hide in case the house was ever burglarized.

Six hours after they started the search, the agents left the house with photographs of Lillian and Donald.

The cane was left behind.

It wasn't listed on the search warrant, which meant they legally couldn't remove it. Under law, only items specified in a warrant can be removed. In this case, investigators could look in a wide range of places for photos since pictures can be well hidden but if agents found other items, such as the cane, they couldn't legally remove them. It was frustrating but it was the law.

Tommy MacDonald and the others were upbeat, though. This was a breakthrough. They were on the way to unraveling the mystery of where Donald Webb had been and, hopefully, where he now was.

The question: was he still alive?

Chapter 8
Working Together

Whenever Massachusetts State Trooper Mike Cherven worked a case, he would check Google to see what odd bits of information about suspects or witnesses might pop up. The internet could provide a wealth of information about people with the stroke of a key. Things like whom their neighbors and friends are, where they went to school, photos on social media of where they vacationed and dined, news stories. Those details could provide insight into a person, put actions into context, and show links in social circles. The case he was now working on in the spring of 2017 was an intricate gaming case and he was curious what might be online about one of the suspects. Carefully, he typed the name into the search engine box.

Stanley Webb.

A story on southcoasttoday.com, the website for the daily newspaper *Standard-Times of New Bedford*, was one of the first to come up. The story detailed Stanley Webb's troubles when he was a New Bedford cop and gave his reasons why, after three years, he left in October of 1983. It talked about his fugitive stepfather, accused of killing a police chief in Pennsylvania and how he quit, feeling fellow officers weren't there to back him up on calls as a result.

Cherven read the article with interest. He had worked in the state police unit assigned to the Bristol District Attorney's Office in New Bedford for seven years before moving to the state Attorney General's Office in Boston in June of 2014 and this was the first he had heard of Donald Eugene Webb.

Cherven then typed "Donald Eugene Webb" into the search engine box. The FBI Most Wanted Fugitive flyer popped up.

A complicated gaming case he was working on just got a bit more intricate.

Over the next few days, after checking with his boss, State Police Lt. Brian Canavan, Mike Cherven called the Pennsylvania State Police contact number on one of the flyers posted online. It was the number of the Butler State Police barracks. He called a few times and eventually connected with Corporal Chris Birckbichler.

"I want to help," Cherven told him.

The Pennsylvania State Police officer was a bit hesitant on the phone. FBI Special Agent Tommy MacDonald was already working the case hard and he didn't know who this new person from Massachusetts was. But the more they talked, the more comfortable Chris felt but he needed to talk more with the FBI—and Tommy MacDonald in particular.

"Let me get your number and call you back," the Pennsylvania investigator said, then called the FBI.

By May of 2017, FBI Special Agent MacDonald was sitting with Massachusetts State Police at the Massachusetts State Attorney General's office, files in hand, to share what he knew so far about the search for Donald Eugene Webb and what had been found in Lillian Webb's basement.

Mike Cherven was surprised at the FBI agent's candor and willingness to work with the Massachusetts troopers. It shattered the stories he and others on the Massachusetts State Police heard for years about the Feds' reluctance to be transparent with local law enforcement on investigations. For several hours, state troopers met with MacDonald and listened to what recently had been done in the case. It was pretty extensive.

After the meeting, Cherven stayed in the office until after two the next morning, reading the copies of the FBI reports

MacDonald left. He was intrigued by the hidden room and cane discovered by the agents. Was there something the Massachusetts state police could do to recover them? Was there something they could do to finally catch Donald Webb?

Cherven earlier had printed out the wanted posters of Donald Eugene Webb off the internet. Throughout the state police office, the face of one of the FBI's Most Wanted men now hung. Is it possible the state police investigation could help find the killer? He hoped so.

In the meantime, Cherven continued work on the gaming case involving the accused killer's stepson. He also tried to find a legal way to retrieve what he believed could be crucial evidence tying Webb to the Dartmouth house.

It would take some time to do it.

Nearly two years after first giving the FBI photos of her family, Mary Ann Jones was in Florida, where she spent half the year. It was springtime and a Monday and she was sitting outside at a local restaurant having dinner with a friend. Her friend, who was in her 70s, worked part-time at a nearby Chick-fil-A and had Mondays off. Except, it turned out, for this particular Monday.

Her friend's phone rang. It was the police. The woman's co-workers called police when she didn't show up for work and asked if they could check her house to make sure she was okay. A neighbor let officers know the woman was out for dinner and police were just confirming. It was a quirky and memorable call for the two women at the time. It was just the start of what was to come later.

When Mary Ann returned home, there was a message waiting. *Call Tommy MacDonald.*

"Do you have any more photos? Let's try this again," he asked her when she called back.

"Let me think about that," Mary Ann answered.

She talked to her youngest son, Greg, that night. Then she talked to her husband, Jim.

Forget the photos, Mary Ann's family told her. Forget appealing to that woman's heart. Let's hit her in the wallet. Let's sue her.

Mary Ann's husband called an attorney in Butler he knew from his work on the school committee by the name of Thomas W. King III. The lawyer agreed to take the case.

On June 1, 2017, the attorney, on behalf of the family, filed a writ of intent to sue in Butler County Common Pleas Court naming Lillian Webb and her son, Stanley Webb, as defendants. The three count civil suit alleged wrongful death-murder; civil conspiracy—accessory after the fact; and civil conspiracy—hindering apprehension of a murderer. They planned to seek more than one million dollars. The attorney planned to ask a judge to let him subpoena and depose Lillian Webb and her son before the actual lawsuit was filed.

It was what Mary Ann called a legal "warning shot" to the Webb family.

Mary Ann wasn't sure if it would hit the target. She figured it would at least make that family uncomfortable.

Once the lawsuit was filed in Pennsylvania, Lillian Webb needed to be formally notified in Massachusetts of the legal action being taken by the family of Greg Adams. Finding Lillian to do that was easy. The FBI "gold team," a group of senior agents tasked with watching the 82-year-old woman, had been following her for months. They watched as she walked her dog in the cemetery, when she went out for coffee, when she went to lunch, when she went to doctor appointments. At any given day, someone on the team lead by Special Agent Charles Prunier knew where she was. Sometimes she tried to lose the tail. Sometimes she didn't.

Things were no different the morning of June 5, 2017, when the "gold team" followed Lillian as she drove through the 97-acre Buttonwood Park in New Bedford. This was the day she was to be served the legal notice about the lawsuit.

FBI Agent Tommy MacDonald, in his black SUV, and a major with the Bristol County Sheriff's department, Floyd Teague, driving a blue unmarked 2011 Crown Victoria cruiser, met behind One Stop Gas at the corner of Kempton and Brownell Streets near the park. Teague hopped in Tommy's SUV where the radio, monitoring the surveillance team, was on. The major had spoken to Tommy several times on the phone but this was the first time the two had met.

Teague listened closely to the radio as the agent drove out from the gasoline station.

The car is leaving the park, the "gold team" radioed.

We are two cars behind her.

She is now was at the intersection.

Tommy and Floyd could see Lillian's car ahead and pulled the SUV behind her. Tommy hit the blue lights. Lillian pulled to the side of the road.

The major got out of the vehicle, holding the court paperwork in one hand, and walked to the driver's side car window.

"You are being served in a civil case," Floyd Teague recalls telling her.

He began to hand her the paperwork. Then she saw the familiar FBI agent round the corner of the SUV.

Lillian took off, her dog in the backseat looking out the side window, down the dead-end Pinett Street. She banged a U-turn, drove towards the FBI SUV and sped off.

They didn't chase her.

There were three reasons why.

One: They were serving paperwork for a civil suit, not arresting her. They could always go to her house.

Two: They didn't want her to get into an accident and injure herself or another person.

Three: If this 82-year-old woman with a yapping dog in the back of her car lost them, their colleagues would never let them live it down.

About a half hour later, the sheriff's department major was at the front door of Lillian's Dartmouth home. No one answered. He left the paperwork tucked into her front door at 11:28 a.m. instead.

The pressure was on Lillian. Again.

While the FBI and Pennsylvania state police were coordinating efforts to find Webb, a retired Rhode Island state police detective named Tommy Denniston was making a few calls of his own during the summer of 2017.

Now a real estate agent in Rhode Island, he never officially worked the case when he was on the job but did run a check through the Rhode Island Registry of Motor Vehicles on the fugitive in 1987 to see if Webb ever had a Rhode Island drivers license and what addresses he gave at the time. He learned Webb was issued a license in July 11, 1972, and it expired in 1980, the year the Chief was killed. Webb gave three different Rhode Island addresses over those years: one in Cranston, one in North Providence and one in Tiverton, a small town just over the Massachusetts state line.

He wrote a report, dated September 27, 1987, on his findings. The search for Webb's records triggered an alert to the FBI and a phone call from an agent, asking why he was looking for the records and asking for whatever information he had. That information needed to go through the Rhode Island State Police chain of command, he said.

Several days later, he said he was called to his supervisor's office, asking why he was looking into Webb, was banned from headquarters and ordered to "never touch another computer."

Denniston said he stopped looking into Webb on his own after that; but after retiring in 2003 at the rank of lieutenant, he eventually began doing some online sleuthing about the fugitive. Eventually he called Jim Poydence in Pennsylvania and the two talked about the case. Denniston told him he suspected the FBI wasn't interested in finding Webb, raised the possibility the fugitive was an informant, and asked if there was a reward in the case. Jim Poydence, who already had extensive conversations with the FBI and whose best friend was a retired FBI agent and one of the original investigators, suggested he talk with Birckbichler from the Pennsylvania State Police.

In his call to Chris Birckbichler, Denniston reiterated his suspicions regarding the FBI and asked about the reward. The reward at that time was $100,000 from the FBI and $5,000 from

Pennsylvania.

Soon after, Denniston said he met with Tommy MacDonald at a Hope Valley, Rhode Island restaurant. By the time of that meeting, Denniston said he had met with a source multiple times who said Lillian Webb was feeling pressured to say where Donald was. He shared that information with the FBI agent. Denniston said he was left with a simple message to relay to his source, who would then talk with Lillian: she could be charged in the case. Denniston believed at the time it likely would be for lying to the FBI.

Not long after the meeting with MacDonald, Denniston was at the US Attorney's office in Rhode Island, meeting with two prosecutors, Paul Daley and William Ferland, Chief of the Criminal Division, along with FBI Special Agent Chris Braga. It was a strange meeting, Braga later recalled. Denniston said he had a source that could help in the case but the person wanted what the FBI agent would later describe as a type of "provisional blanket, unnamed immunity" first. The source wanted immunity for all, unspecified crimes. Denniston wouldn't name the source or say what information the person had.

The prosecutors rejected the offer. It was not how things were done. Unless the source came forward and the information could be confirmed, there would be no deal—and no reward, Braga recalled Denniston was told.

Tommy MacDonald tried unsuccessfully to get a second federal search warrant to retrieve the cane and other possible evidence from the hidden room. The first search warrant for photographs of Donald Webb gave the agents wide latitude on where to look. Photos can be anywhere: in a drawer, under a bed, in a closet, shuffled in a stack of papers, in a desk, hidden behind a secret panel. There wasn't enough evidence—or probable cause—to legally get back in again in this decades old murder case, he was told. He needed more evidence.

The FBI agent didn't give up. The investigation had gotten this far. There had to be a way to legally get back in the house, get the cane and other items, such as the hidden room door, and test them for Donald Webb's DNA. To Tommy Mac-Donald, that secret room was evidence that the killer had been hiding in the house. The room was the perfect size for Webb to slip into if anyone, including a police officer, came into the finished basement. The agent was convinced evidence in that room would answer the decades old question: where did Webb hide?

Tommy MacDonald returned to the state police investigators at the state Attorney General's office for help. There had to be a way to get another search warrant for the house.

Massachusetts State Trooper Mike Cherven, who as homicide investigator in the Bristol County District Attorney's Office handled the homicide case involving Patriots football player Aaron Hernandez, talked with one of his bosses, Lt. Brian Canavan, about what could be done. Let's look at the case differently, the trooper suggested. Let's not look at this as a federal fugitive case but as an active murder investigation.

Cherven and Canavan were already part of the team working on what was the largest gaming investigation in Massachusetts targeting Stanley Webb, who was Donald's stepson, and the younger Webb's company, Nutel Communications. The case was the second investigation launched under the state's new, expanded gaming and money laundering laws created in 2011, and it was massive.

There was a wiretap on six cell phones, examination of financial records, GPS monitoring, physical surveillance and all the things that go into plain old good police work—but on a larger scale. The team was already deep into that investigation when Cherven and Canavan approached two prosecutors in the Attorney General's Office, Patrick Hanley, Chief of the AG's Gaming Enforcement Division, and Kimberly West, head of the AG's Criminal Bureau, with a request.

"Can we obtain a warrant for Lillian's house?"

They got the green light.

But the search at Lillian's house needed to be delayed for a bit.

On June 27, 2017, the team executed 103 search warrants

obtained a day earlier in the Nutel gaming probe to seize financial records, slot machines and bank accounts. It was a massive multi-level undertaking.

The operation involved more than 300 police officers and led to the seizure of more than $2.1 million, including $450,000 hidden in a compartment at Stanley Webb's Westport, Massachusetts home. In the case, prosecutors alleged 130 illegal casino-like gambling machines were placed near Massachusetts State Lottery products in different locations, including gasoline stations and social clubs and were programmed so it was near impossible for anyone to win.

As police were executing the search warrants, Stanley Webb's daughter was caught on the wiretap telling her sister to burn all the evidence relating to Nutel and the gaming machines.

State Police also obtained a separate search warrant for Lillian's house at the same time but the Nutel investigation needed so many resources that investigators just didn't have enough manpower to hit her home that day. But they didn't wait long.

One day after state police executed the search warrants in connection with Stanley Webb's business, and three weeks after the civil suit notice was left, the state police came knocking on Lillian's door.

Lillian Webb sat at her dining room table. Pennsylvania State Police Corporal Chris Birckbichler was to her right at the corner. Trooper Max DeLuca was next to him. The three could hear the commotion in the finished basement, where a team of Massachusetts state police officers, led by Trooper Mike Cherven, were removing the door from that hidden room FBI agents discovered seven months earlier.

It was June 28, 2017, 23 days after the civil suit was filed and one day after police raided the business owned by Lillian's son. The Massachusetts State Police, working with the Pennsylvania State Police, had obtained a second search warrant two days earlier in Boston Municipal Court, a warrant granted by Assistant Clerk Mark J. Concannon. It was based on the observations of the FBI agents back in November of 2016 and it allowed them to seize what the federal agents couldn't: the hidden room door, the cane, the coins and anything else that could prove Donald Webb had been in the house. Any DNA found on the cane, the door or anywhere else could be compared with the DNA profile finally obtained from blood samples collected inside that getaway car Webb used back in 1980.

The team of investigators from the Pennsylvania State Police, Massachusetts State Police, and analysts from the State Police Crime Lab were now at 28 Maplecrest Drive and hoping to finally close the case.

As the two Pennsylvania state police officers sat at the table, they were convinced this would be their first—and last— shot to get Lillian to break, to finally say where the killer of Greg Adams was.

Chris Birckbichler was warned how not to approach Lillian. "She doesn't like publicity. She considers herself much younger than her 80-plus years. She pictures herself as a young lady. Don't treat her as a senior citizen. Don't call her 'ma'am.' Coming at her hard likely won't work."

Chris considered that advice—and ignored it the moment he got to the house.

"Ma'am, we would like to talk with you," Chris told her.

Then he escalated his questioning.

He kept asking: where is Donald Webb.

She kept answering: I don't know.

He pressed a bit harder.

I appreciate you talking with us but we are going to keep coming back until you tell us where he is, Chris told her.

"I don't know where he is. I don't know," she answered, he recalled.

"Let's pick a date," he told her. "That's when we will be back. Between my partner, Max, here and myself, we will keep coming back."

"I don't know where he is."

"This is going to continue until we find him," Chris answered. "We are going to keep coming at you until we find him."

Max played soft to his partner's tough.

It didn't seem to work.

She lowered her eyes. "I don't know where he is," the investigators recalled her saying.

Max noticed, as they talked, she kept rising from her chair, peering out the back window or the rear door into the backyard. "Where is my dog?" She asked each time. "Where is my dog?"

Chris ignored her and pressed again. "We are going to keep putting cop cars in your front yard. We are not giving up. We are not going away."

"I don't know anything," she answered, lowering her eyes again, the investigators recalled.

"Your neighbors will wonder what's going on. Just tell us where Donald is. Just tell us where Donald is."

"I don't know anything."

"You can go back to your private life. Just tell us where he is."

"I don't know anything. I don't know."

"Lillian, he was an evil man," Chris remembers telling her. "If you killed him because he mouthed off at you, I don't care. If he died like a dog, I don't care. I want him."

"I don't know anything," she repeated yet again. "I don't know where he is."

Downstairs, Massachusetts State Police were taking several items as evidence: the door to the hidden room, the doorframe, the door latch, the black cane inside, some coins. All of the items would be processed for DNA, blood, fibers and other evidence. All of the items would be compared with the DNA profile of Donald Eugene Webb. Any fingerprints would be compared with the Webb's prints on file.

Massachusetts State Trooper Mike Cherven walked from the basement through the garage and outside, with the door to the hidden room on his shoulder wrapped up. The investigators inside told Lillian to take note of what the trooper was carrying. DNA doesn't go away, Cherven was later told.

Hours after walking into the Maplecrest home, Chris Birckbichler and Max DeLuca left, dejected, with their Massachusetts counterparts.

As the two boarded the flight from T.F. Green Airport in Rhode Island to Pittsburgh that night, they were now convinced Lillian Webb would never tell them where the killer of Chief Adams was.

They had come so close.

This, they felt, was the end of the investigation.

The wooden door taken from the hidden room in Lillian's basement was brought to the state police crime laboratory in Lakeville, Massachusetts where it would be examined for fingerprints. The pores on the ridges of the fingers contain sweat pores and it is that sweat, and the residue it contains, which form fingerprint impressions on items. If your finger touches a surface, the sweat is transferred to the surface in a way that replicates the ridge patterns of the finger. Usually, you don't see it with the naked eye because sweat is colorless. But the impressions it makes—called latent fingerprints—can be developed and viewed through a chemical process using a Super Glue-like substance called cyanoacrylate.

What happens is an item, such as the door, is placed inside a large specialized chamber where the humidity is adjusted and the cyanoacrylate is heated. When the cyanoacrylate is heated, it creates a gas that circulates inside the chamber. The resulting gas binds to the moisture and residue left behind from the sweat and reveals any latent fingerprints left behind.

Exactly who developed the method is open to debate. In the late 1970s, researchers in the United Kingdom and Japan are believed to have nearly simultaneously developed the method—and in one case by accident.

L.W. Wood from the Northampton Police in United Kingdom was repairing a film tank with Superglue when he noticed his own fingerprints were developed on the tank. Wood later reported the findings to the Home Office. But it is Masato Soba from the Saga Prefectural Crime Laboratory of the National Police Agency of Japan who is believed to be the first to intentionally use the method after learning a colleague, Fueeo Matsumura, discovered his own prints on a slide while examining a hair in a murder case. Another scientist, Louis Bourdon, in July of 1980, of Ontario, Canada also is believed to have uncovered by the method on his own.

The U.S. Army learned of the method after it was used in 1978 by the Japanese National Police Agency, and brought it to the United States. It was later used in the laboratory of the Bureau of Alcohol, Tobacco and Firearms.

Since the late 1970s and early 1980s, the so-called "Superglue" method for the development of latent fingerprints has been used throughout the world. In Massachusetts, it was used regularly.

Massachusetts State Trooper David Mackin wasn't sure what he and others in the Crime Services unit would uncover when they placed the door from the Dartmouth house into the lab unit to be fumed.

It didn't take long before the testing revealed some fingerprints.

The fingerprints were those of Donald Eugene Webb.

Additional tests to uncover and identify any DNA samples were also successful. The DNA found inside the room was also that of Webb.

They now knew where the killer had been. But where was he now?

The day after the State Police search, the FBI Gold Team watched as Lillian left her home and drove to her lawyer's office on Federal Hill in Providence, Rhode Island, roughly 40 minutes away.

Charles Prunier, the team leader, reported her location back to the office.

Authorities didn't know for sure why she was there or

what she told her attorney. However, it was an intriguing turn in the case. Maybe the search for Donald Webb hadn't reached a dead end.

It was a few days after returning from Massachusetts, and Max DeLuca was discouraged. It was over. They would never find Webb. This had been the best shot at finding the accused killer and it fell short. They drew on the resources of the FBI, state police in Pennsylvania and Massachusetts and even law enforcement retirees. They tried to appeal to Lillian Webb's sympathy for the Chief's family. She was followed. She was interviewed by federal and state investigators. She was threatened with a civil suit. Her house was searched twice. But, even after all that, Lillian wouldn't budge.

DeLuca was trying to shake off the disappointment as he strode one morning in early July into the Butler State Police barracks on the hill overlooking New Castle Road. He walked up to his second floor office and then checked the mail for his crime unit 50 feet down the hall. There was a white envelope in the cubby like mail slot addressed to him. The return address was Atwells Avenue in Providence. It was Lillian's attorney.

He walked into his office, sat down and slit open the envelope. *He's going to say leave my client alone,* DeLuca thought. *Stay away.*

DeLuca began to read the single-page letter, dated June 29, 2017 and postmarked June 30.

I represent Lillian C. Webb regarding an investigation which you are conducting. I have written to first Assistant District Attorney Patrice J. McLean.

It is my hope that the case can be resolved and that it will involve a deposition. At that time, I would like you to bring the photographs and other personal items seized on December 16, 2016; and the $10,000 in U.S. currency, the gold coins and the 50c pieces seized on June 28, 2017.

I appreciate your giving attention to my request.

Sincerely,
John F. Cicilline

Max called Assistant District Attorney Patricia J. McLean immediately.

It all did work, he thought. *It may finally end.*

Patrick Hanley, Assistant Attorney General in Massachusetts, received a similar letter from the defense attorney and contacted one of the prosecutors in the Bristol County District Attorney's Office, Patrick Bomberg. "There might be a resolution," he told him.

Two weeks after the search on Maplecrest Drive, the prosecutors in Butler, Pennsylvania, and the Attorney General's office in Boston were on a conference call on July 12, 2017, with the defense attorney in Providence, Jack Cicilline.

Lillian would talk.

The terms were simple: Lillian would be granted immunity from prosecution in Massachusetts and Pennsylvania for harboring a fugitive and the civil suit filed in Pennsylvania would be dropped. Butler County Assistant District Attorney Patricia J. McLean drafted one letter, granting Lillian immunity in Pennsylvania. Assistant Attorney General Patrick Hanley and Bomberg, the Bristol County prosecutor, crafted a second granting Lillian immunity in Massachusetts. It is illegal to lie to the FBI, but federal prosecutors decided not to pursue those charges, even though a formal immunity agreement was not given.

It was an easy deal to make for prosecutors in both states to make. It wasn't illegal for spouses to harbor a fugitive wife or husband in Massachusetts and Lillian didn't hide her husband in Pennsylvania. In Massachusetts, under Chapter 274 Section 12, being a spouse of a fugitive is a defense against a criminal harboring charge. Massachusetts Assistant Attorney General Patrick Hanley knew this when presented with the terms. They would be giving her immunity for crimes she couldn't be prosecuted for. However, neither the state prosecutors in Pennsylvania nor in Massachusetts told her that. All they said was: It's a deal.

It was then up to the Adams family to make a decision.

The $1 million civil suit by the Adams family was filed in Pennsylvania to force her to finally say where Webb was. Since Lillian didn't commit a crime in Pennsylvania, it was considered near impossible to hold her liable civilly in that state. It appeared, though, the mere threat of this civil suit—and potentially losing property and money—was working when a criminal charge couldn't. At the time, Lillian owned at least two properties with her son, one on Hawthorn Street in New Bedford and the other on Maplecrest Drive house in Dartmouth where she lived. Those houses, assessed at a total of roughly $600,000, would be safe from a civil suit filed by the family. So would be any bank accounts or other assets in Lillian's name.

The agreement by the slain chief's family to drop the suit turned out to be the needed leverage to get answers. The family of Chief Adams decided finding an answer was worth it.

Butler County District Attorney Richard Goldinger would later say Lillian was under intense pressure from law enforcement and her own son to say where Donald was. Stanley was under investigation in Massachusetts as part of a probe into illegal gaming and the search for his stepfather was getting to him. Investigators believed, based on information they gathered, the son was putting pressure on his mother.

"He said to her, 'You're going to pick him over me?' Or something to that effect," Goldinger recalled. "The son didn't know if he (Donald Webb) was dead or not."

While things now seemed to be moving quickly, those close to the case were trying not to raise hopes. Butler County prosecutors and investigators had been down this circuitous road before. They wanted specifics from Lillian Webb and they wanted to know exactly where the killer was. They wanted Donald.

Once the agreements to drop the civil suit and to grant immunity were reached, the defense attorney provided some information about what Lillian would say: Donald was long dead and he was buried in her backyard.

Tommy MacDonald was eating breakfast at Becky's Diner in Portland, Maine after serving a warrant on another case early that morning when his cellphone rang. It was Pennsylvania State Police Corporal Chris Birckbichler.

"You have to step outside. We have to talk," Birckbichler told him.

Lillian was officially willing to cooperate. Donald Eugene Webb was dead. She would say where he was buried.

Tommy always harbored the hope that Webb was alive and would stand trial for murder. He wanted a call saying the killer was in custody. This would have to do.

News that Webb was dead wasn't a complete surprise to Tommy. There were several indications he wasn't alive. One former cohort of Webb's referred to him in the past tense during an interview. There was that church bulletin found in Lillian's house announcing the Mass for Webb and there were the palm crosses tucked into the photo frame with Webb's photo.

Tommy also wasn't surprised by the news that Lillian would cooperate. He knew about the discussions the state prosecutors were having and immunity letters that were drafted. He knew that would only happen if an agreement was near, one that would end the search.

In Massachusetts, the FBI and Massachusetts State Police scrambled to organize a dig for the next day. A surveillance camera, trained on Lillian's house for some time, would give investigators a heads up if anyone tried to move anything from the site before they got there. Trooper Mike Cherven put together a search warrant for the property, weaving information from what was discovered earlier by the FBI and affidavits from Pennsylvania State Troopers Max DeLuca and Chris Birckbichler, now a corporal. He then walked the two blocks from his office at the state Attorney General's office to the Boston Police Department's District A1 station where an on-call clerk magistrate was setting bail for arrestees.

"I need a search warrant," he told the clerk magistrate,

Justyna Miller.

She initially scanned the warrant affidavit. Cherven saw her jaw drop. This was not a routine search warrant. They moved into the record room where the clerk read the affidavit carefully before signing it. Step one for the dig was done.

While Cherven was preparing the warrant, other troopers were buying shovels. Step two for the dig.

Calls went out to the District Attorney's Office in Bristol County, the Saxonburg Police Department and FBI and Pennsylvania State Police retirees who worked the case in those early days. Don't tell anyone but do you want to be here? Step three.

The walls of the narrow basement lobby of the Saxonburg police department are lined with photos of Greg Adams, newspaper stories and his posthumous awards. There is the plaque: "In loving memory of Chief of Police Gregory B. Adams, served as a friend, professional and dedicated officer, fatally wounded while on duty, Dec. 4, 1980."

There is a framed photo from 1976 of two men, Adams, then an officer, and Saxonburg Police Chief James Grady side by side. There is the 1984 calendar with his photo. There is his hat. There is an award from the National Society of the Sons of the American Revolution. There is his business card, framed. There are news clippings about the case. There is a framed poem, honoring all of the Saxonburg chiefs.

Decades after Chief Adams was beaten and shot to death, these walls still speak to that December afternoon and what the community lost. December 4, 1980, is a day frozen in wooden frames, told in news clippings and photographs. A law enforcement life honored with citations.

The Saxonburg municipal building has been renovated since 1980. The first floor courtroom has moved into an office building down the street and across the way. The police department later moved into the basement of the municipal building, the same place State Police investigators had set up a makeshift office in 1980 after the killing.

Joseph Beachem was 12 years old and living 30 miles from Saxonburg when the Chief was killed. He grew up hearing his parents talk about the murder and the search for the killer. By the time he became a police officer in 2010 and later became Chief in Saxonburg, he could feel how intertwined the Chief's death was in the town's psyche. Saxonburg is a tightknit Pennsylvania borough with a quaint downtown and sprawling outskirts. Memories ran deep and as long as the coldest winter. Each December, the community lays a wreath at the memorial bearing an image of the fallen chief outside the municipal building. Each December, the pain of that 1980 afternoon surfaces. Each December, residents wondered if this was the year Donald Eugene Webb would be caught. Then the January cold sets in and another year passes.

When FBI Special Agent Tommy MacDonald first contacted Pennsylvania State Police Corporal Chris Birckbichler in 2015 and, later, the Saxonburg Chief about the case, Beachem was cautiously hopeful. He was heartened no one forgot Greg Adams' killer was still a fugitive. But his optimism was tempered. Over the years, Beachem received occasional updates about Webb sightings that turned out to be false and tips that fell short. This did seem to be different, though. After 2015, when he first heard from Chris Birckbichler, Beachem got the sense something would finally happen.

Beachem heard snippets about the renewed investigation—nothing too specific. Just enough to know the case was still moving forward. He was called after the FBI searched Lillian Webb's Dartmouth home in 2016. He was called after the Massachusetts State Police searched the house again in June. He knew Greg Adams' family was suing Lillian, hoping that would force the woman to give up the accused killer's location.

Still, when the final call came, it was a surprise.

It came late around 7 p.m. on July 12, 2017.

It was from Birckbichler.

"We think we located Webb," Birckbichler said. "There is going to be an excavation tomorrow. Would you like to be there?"

When a cop killer is caught, the dead officer's handcuffs are traditionally snapped on the suspect's wrists. It happened earlier that year, in January of 2017, when the handcuffs of slain Orlando, Florida, Police Lieutenant Debra Clayton were used when the man accused of killing her was arrested. It was done a year later when the killer of Weymouth, Massachusetts, Police Sergeant Michael Chesna was taken to court.

The handcuffs are a symbolic gesture. So would be the sight of a Saxonburg police cruiser outside a Massachusetts home as members of law enforcement took turns digging to find the bones of Donald Eugene Webb. Justice from the grave. The bond of blue is eternal. So is justice.

Beachem was told to keep quiet about what would happen the next day. No one outside a tight circle could know. The only person he called was the Mayor. He needed to let him know he was taking the cruiser out of state.

Mayor William Gillespie was about 25 minutes away in north central Butler County, at the grand opening of the new Double A Golf Shop, a business owned by a friend. The business had relocated to a new spot and the Mayor, his wife and youngest son, Thomas, who had worked for the golf shop owners, were on hand to help their friends celebrate.

Chief Beachem was direct when the Mayor answered the phone. "Can you come to the station?"

"What's going on?"

"I would rather wait until you get here to explain," the Chief answered.

The Mayor hung up and turned to his wife. "I have to go. Thomas will take you home."

His wife asked what happened. "I can't say," he told her.

Less than a half-hour later, the Mayor pulled into the police department parking lot and walked into Chief Beachem's office.

"They may have found Chief Adams' killer," Beachem told him.

He gave the Mayor the basic information he had: the killer apparently was buried in a Massachusetts yard, police would be digging Webb up the next day and state police would really like a Saxonburg police cruiser to be outside the house during the digging.

The Mayor gave him the go-ahead, with one caveat.

"I would like to go with you," the Mayor said.

So, that night, the Mayor and the Chief told their wives they had to drive to New England and would be back some-time, hopefully, the next day. They said they would explain why later. The Chief took the marked SUV Explorer cruiser and met the Mayor in a business parking lot in Cranberry Township just north of Saxonburg around one in the morning. The Mayor left his car there and the two drove 11 hours north in the Saxonburg Police Department SUV. They didn't stop.

Once they hit New England, the cruiser hugged the coast-al Interstate 95 through Connecticut and up to Providence, Rhode Island before heading east onto Interstate 195 toward Massachusetts. The sights were beautiful, they would later say.

Originally, the two were to meet investigators at the Mas-sachusetts State Police barracks off Faunce Corner Road in Dartmouth, a light brown building down the road from the county jail. The barracks, opened in 2006, replaced the historic white clapboard house that served the State Police D Troop since 1920. But the dig was moving faster than expected and Beachem got a call just as they crossed the line into Rhode Is-land: go right to the house.

Beachem typed 28 Maplecrest Drive, Dartmouth, Massa-chusetts, into the map app on his iPhone and sped up.

Chapter 9
Answers

They crowded around the dining room table in the Maplecrest Drive, Dartmouth home. Lillian with her attorney, John F. Cicilline, and his son, John M. Cicilline, also an attorney. The retired Rhode Island state trooper named Tom Denniston who said a source (he declined to name the person) asked him to join Lillian and the defense attorneys at the house.

FBI agents Tommy MacDonald and Donald Kornek. Pennsylvania State Police Corporal Chris Birckbichler and Max DeLuca. Massachusetts Troopers Mike Cherven, Michael Tryon and Sgt. Kevin Baker. There were a few others standing behind them, listening. Outside, a team of troopers and FBI agents waited. Some had shovels. They knew what they would be doing that day.

The investigators agreed Chris Birckbichler would lead the interview with Lillian. He and Max DeLuca flew in from Pennsylvania and had only spoken with her once. They all figured she was tired of talking with the FBI agents—and with Tommy MacDonald in particular, the man who knocked on her door for so many years.

Chris looked across the table at Lillian. He asked if he could record her. She agreed.

"The first question, the most important question on everybody's mind is: Where's Don?"

"He is on the property," she answered.

She sketched out, on a piece of paper, a crude map. He was in the backyard, buried roughly four feet deep, she told them.

Then, as the investigators listened, injecting occasionally with questions, she told the story of how he got there.

It was December of 1980, and Donald pulled up to her mother's home on McCabe Street in the white Cougar. Lillian was outside with a girlfriend, heading to her car when she saw him. He told Lillian he was hurt. Lillian's girlfriend, who was a nurse, looked at Donald's injuries. His left ankle seemed to be shattered. Part of his bottom lip appeared to be ripped off. The injuries, he would later tell his wife, occurred in the life-and-death struggle with a cop in the parking lot in Saxonburg. The Chief, who had a black belt in karate, fought hard that day. The Chief kicked, he punched and he bit off part of Donald's lip. Donald was bleeding so badly at the scene that later investigators, wrongly, had been convinced he had been shot.

Lillian looked at her husband's injuries and knew what he needed to do. "I said, 'You have to go to the hospital,'" she recounted to investigators.

They drove to Tobey Hospital, a small community hospital in the coastal town of Wareham about 25 minutes away nicknamed "the Gateway to the Cape," Lillian in one car with her girlfriend, Webb in the Cougar. There, Webb was admitted under the alias "John Thomas" for treatment. The doctors were told he hurt his leg while "in the mountains."

Lillian told them she later drove the Cougar to a motel lot in Warwick, Rhode Island, far enough from her home but close enough for police to find. She adjusted the mirrors and pushed the driver's seat back so it would appear a taller person, likely a man, had driven it there. Another one of her girlfriends had sneaked out of a ballet to follow her to Rhode Island and bring her back to Massachusetts. Her friend then went back to the ballet. "She had to go back there so no one would know," Lillian told investigators.

She said the point of leaving the car in the motel parking lot was to throw off investigators, figuring police would be watching to see who would pick it up. "I put it where you could really see it … I kept them really busy for awhile."

Police found cigarette butts in the back seat ashtray of the Cougar, Chris Birckbichler told her. "Whose cigarettes were in the back?" he asked.

She insisted she didn't know. "He was alone. He said he was not with anyone else," Lillian answered.

After Lillian ditched the car, Donald stayed in that Wareham hospital under the assumed name for three weeks, recovering. When he was released, she told him he couldn't stay with her in New Bedford because her son was at the house. Instead, Donald moved into a rooming house, likely in the seaside village of Onset in Wareham, Massachusetts, a community just before one of the bridges to Cape Cod. "Right across from the water. It was a nice place, one room," she told the investigators.

She was vague on how long he stayed at the rooming house or exactly where in town it was. While there, he would call her during the day on the 800 number at Alden Corrugated, the factory where she worked, and the couple would make arrangements to meet. If she detected a FBI or State Police tail she couldn't shake, she would head back home. If she eluded the agents, she would meet him. There always seemed to be someone following her. She told them about the time she was driving to meet Donald and spotted an agent behind her.

"I was on the outside passing lane and I was being followed, and he was on the inside lane and I waited until he went straight and I went to the shopping mall and I parked the car because I knew he would be back … He was shocked I was waiting for him to come. I waved and then I took off. I didn't want to get him too mad," she said.

When she moved from her second-floor apartment on 29 Carriage Drive in New Bedford to a house on Hawthorne Street in early 1981 after her son moved out, Donald moved in—first into the garage, then the basement, she told investigators.

"He slept there. He stayed there. There was a table and chairs. There was a TV there and a bathroom and the laundry where I used to do the laundry," she said.

However, Donald wasn't always in the basement or at home. He would come and go from her house; she insisted she was never sure where he went. She didn't provide exact dates or times. Occasionally, though, she would drive him to doctors and a dentist in Wareham. She told investigators she didn't remember the names or the addresses.

Tommy MacDonald asked about those times when FBI agents saw her drive into the garage, the automatic door barely missing the rear of the car as it came down. Was Don in the vehicle at those times? "Probably," she answered, her voice light.

She told them there was a time when Brockton, Massachusetts police picked up Webb in that city, roughly 25 miles south of Boston. The officers didn't know he was wanted and they never took his fingerprints. "They thought he was crazy, he tried to commit suicide or something," she said. "They didn't take prints or anything. If they did they would have known."

Instead, Webb, likely again using the alias John Thomas, was taken to a hospital—either in Brockton or nearby, she said. He called her and she picked him up, bringing him back to her home on Hawthorne Street.

Her son, Stanley, had moved out by then. It was just Lillian and Donald in the house. No one knew her husband was there, she insisted. "Stan was busy with his girlfriend. I made sure no one was there except the dogs and myself," she said.

Donald came and went, sometimes staying away for weeks or months. She was vague on the times. Sometimes, she said, she would come home and he would be gone. She said she didn't know how he left, where he went or if he had a car. She used to give him large amounts of money—roughly $5,000 at a time.

Did he ever watch any of the television programs featuring the case, such as *America's Most Wanted*? FBI Agent MacDonald asked.

"No, he shut that off," she answered.

She insisted Donald felt bad about what happened, even

once talking about turning himself in. He never did.

The investigators broached the subject of Florida, where the FBI once got a tip Webb was hiding out with a buddy. Did he ever go there while on the run, she was asked. Did he ever come back from those absences with a tan?

Lillian told them she didn't think he ever went to Florida, even though she repeatedly said she wasn't sure where he went when he left her house in those early months and years. She said she didn't believe he did any criminal jobs or had any contact with Frank Lach, his former partner in crime, once he went into hiding.

"Frankie Lach and he had a falling out a long time ago," she said.

Lach didn't know where Webb was, she said. "There was no way he would know. I didn't speak to him and Don didn't speak to him as far as I know." The others who claimed to know where Webb was over the years likely were lying, police were told.

"Did he have a second life outside of you? Did he have a wife or girlfriend?" agent Tommy MacDonald asked.

"Not that I know of," she answered.

Eventually, Lillian told them, she moved from the house on Hawthorn Street in New Bedford to the Dartmouth house in 1997. Donald came with her. The new house was also under surveillance, she knew.

Birckbichler asked her: "You were able to get him in and out of the house without being seen?"

"Yes," she answered.

"No interaction with any of the neighbors. Nothing like that?"

"No."

Birckbichler pressed slightly. "Lillian, let me ask this. He was out, he was being seen at the doctor, he was seen amongst people. There had to be a tremendous amount of press, on the news, about him. He had distinctive tattoos and a look. Was there ever concern?"

Lillian answered quickly, "He didn't have distinctive tattoos. He had his name on one hand, left or right I don't' know, it was *Don* and it was very light. And he had *Ann* on his chest."

"So he never did anything to take those to take those off, to hide them?" Birckbichler asked.

"No. Put makeup on them, I don't know. Erase or something like that," she answered, referring to a makeup cover-up popular at that time.

She insisted her husband rarely left the Dartmouth house after that move from New Bedford and no one knew he was at her new home.

"Your son never knew?" Birckbichler asked.

"My son, no. Hey, he would have told everybody," she answered.

"How about your brother?"

One source earlier had told investigators Lillian's brother knew where Webb was.

"No, absolutely not. My brother would have told his girl or somebody," she told the Pennsylvania trooper.

"I can't hide a thing in my house how do you manage to do that for years and years and years?" Chris asked.

"I did. I did," she insisted.

She told the investigators that when she played cards upstairs with her girlfriends, Donald would be in the basement.

No one ever knew he was there, she insisted.

A secret shared was no secret.

She never told the investigators who built the hidden room found in the basement by the FBI. She first insisted it was there when she moved in. She then told investigators she had someone build the closet before she moved in and it wasn't constructed very well. She refused to say it was the place where Donald hid, even though his DNA and a cane were found there. The previous owners told authorities the secret space was not there when they sold the house. (Investigators believe Webb planned to hide there if anyone came to the house, particularly police.)

For roughly an hour, the investigators listened as she talked in broad and general terms of her hidden life with Donald, peppering in a few specifics.

They listened as she talked more about the injury to his

leg that crippled him for life during that fatal confrontation with Chief Adams.

The Chief fought hard for his life. He kicked. He bit. He punched.

Part of Donald Webb's lip was ripped off. His lower leg was broken so severely the ankle was fused, leaving him with a painful gait.

Tommy MacDonald asked her about the state police lieutenant working at the District Attorney's Office, Gordon Clarkson, whom everyone believed tipped her off about the hunt for Webb shortly after the killing.

"Gordon Clarkson said to me Don may have been, may have been, involved in a shooting of a police chief and if he contacts me, he said, let us know. And I said, 'Yeah, I will,'" she told them. "That was Gordon Clarkson that told me that. He was with the state police detectives."

The District Attorney at the time, Ronald Pina, lived in her previous New Bedford neighborhood and Lillian said she would often go for walks in the area. "I used to walk by his house and he didn't know who I was," she said. "He didn't know who he was saying 'hi' to." She said years later, when Pina represented her in her divorce from Webb after her husband died, she kidded him about those encounters on the street.

She ribbed FBI Agent Tommy MacDonald, who had asked her during that first search about the painting of Webb on the wall in the house. He had asked her if it was Donald. She said no at the time. Now, sitting at the table, she noted with a lilt in her voice that it wasn't Donald, it was a picture of Donald. Carefully chosen words in a decades-long game of cat and mouse, the investigators knew.

The investigators listened as she told them about her husband's first stroke in 1997, about his infirmities, how he spent most his time in bed after that stroke.

"He couldn't stand and I gave him a ball to strengthen up his hands but he couldn't do anything," she said.

Birckbichler asked if Webb was paralyzed on one side from the stroke.

"All of it, it was not one side. Whatever was wrong with him, it was all over. He could not move. He could talk," she said.

"And he stayed in the basement?" he asked.

"No."

"Up here?"

"Yeah. I couldn't get him downstairs."

She told them she suspected the end was near as 1999 came to a close. She said the two had talked about what to do when he died. He told her to dig a hole in the backyard. She would bury him there. No one would know.

As Donald's health continued to decline that year, Lillian would go into the yard and slowly dig into the frozen soil. It was tough at first but once she got through the frozen topsoil it got easier, she said. It took about three weeks, alone at night, to prepare the four-foot-long, four-foot-deep grave, she told investigators. "I didn't want to bother anybody and I didn't want to involve anybody so I did it," she said.

By the time Donald died, the grave was ready.

It was December 30, 1999, a Thursday, the night before New Year's Eve. She went out for dinner with a girlfriend. It wasn't long after she returned home that Webb died. It was around 9:35 p.m. She said she knew she had to act quickly.

"I didn't want his body to smell. I got very nervous with that because I had dogs, two dogs. And I said, 'I have to get him out of the house,'" she told the investigators.

She said she took a blanket to help cover him, placed his body in a large green plastic storage bin and dragged the container down the three stairs from the bedroom to the first floor of the raised ranch then to the backyard. She flipped his body out of the tote and into the hole she had spent weeks digging. She looked down into the hole at her husband.

"His eyes were open and I tried to shut them and I couldn't," she said. "So I said, 'God don't let him be alive.' But he was dead."

Then she began to cover the body. She dragged lime from the shed and poured it on the body. Then some stones. Then dirt. She found topsoil she used for gardening to help fill the hole. She tried to be quiet.

"I was nervous. I didn't want anyone to see me and it was late at night and I didn't want any noise," she said.

She kept the tote she used to drag Donald to the grave. She threw out the blanket, she said.

When the FBI first searched her home, the agents found church bulletins from a Fall River Catholic parish. Two Masses for a Donald Webb in 2006 were listed. Why a Fall River church? Tommy asked her. "You live in North Dartmouth."

Lillian explained she picked the Fall River church because the priest had a girlfriend who was the sister-in-law of one of her friends. "They go off together all the time," she said. "I said, 'Well, keep him busy. Let him say Mass. Maybe he will remember that he has to keep all his vows.'"

Lillian insisted neither she nor Donald considered themselves religious but they both went to Catholic schools.

"And I believe in God and I believe in prayer and I prayed this time to Virgin Mary because that's who I believe in. She helped me. We are here. I have to end this," she said.

She was asked if there was a reason why she was finally talking to investigators, finally giving Donald Webb up.

"To end this, I want it to be over with. I can't take it. I just can't. I can't sleep, I don't sleep. I haven't slept one night all night long. I haven't. Every time I get up I look out the window to see if you guys are around. You are on my mind all the time. I can't live with that."

Investigators told her the backyard search was likely to be lengthy. Did she want to leave? Did she want to go to a hotel? Did she want to stay with her son?

"No," she answered each time. She would stay.

Then the interview was over.

"Ready for the walk?" her attorney asked.

She stood up, walked to the back door and then outside. The investigators pushed back their chairs and followed.

She turned slightly to the left in the backyard near a shed and pointed to a small bench. "He's there," she told them and turned to return to the house.

FBI agent Tommy MacDonald stopped her.

"Show us exactly where," he insisted.

Lillian stepped back to the shed and to a spot between the shed, fence and bench.

Investigators lifted the wooden bench.

With the toe of her foot, she drew a line in the dirt. The line stretched the full length of the shed and two feet out.

"He is right here," she told them, investigators recalled.

She walked away.

Now, the work began.

The investigators cleared the yard as Trooper E. Timothy Blackwell came in with his specially trained K-9, Klaas. Blackwell slipped a one-and-a-half-inch leather collar on the dog, the signal to the canine the search was for a body, before leading the five-year-old Belgian Malinois through the right side of the fenced yard.

"Bones," the trooper told the dog.

Klaas abruptly turned to the left and ran to the shed. At the spot where Lillian drew a line in the dirt, the dog stopped. First, he defecated less than a foot away. Then the dog began barking at a tree inches from the suspected grave before sitting down, the signal he found something.

"Good boy," Blackwell said, pulling out a reward for the dog—a tug toy to play with.

Massachusetts State Trooper David Mackin took photos of the spot. The forensic anthropologist, James Pokines, came in to examine it, offering advice on how best to dig. He first stuck a metal probe into the dirt to check the consistency of the ground. Generally, at a grave site the ground surrounding a body will be softer and disrupted.

Then the investigators lined up and began to shovel under Pokines' direction. Painstakingly slow and carefully.

First they found a gun. A white handled .22-caliber revolver. Tommy MacDonald, as he looked at the weapon, remembered a retired agent, Jack McGraw, told him Webb always carried a small gun.

Then they found the empty bag of lime.

They dug through a layer of lime—Lillian told them she put it there to cut down on the smell. They dug past some stones.

They used an axe to cut the thick roots now woven through the makeshift grave. They used power tools. They took turns, in pairs, digging and chopping and cutting. Cherven, Mackin, Sgt. William Tarbokas and FBI Agent Richard Pires. Sweat soaked their clothes.

As the hole got deeper, FBI Agent Pires climbed in, removing dirt using what looked like a red plastic pail. The dirt was run through a screen to catch bone fragments or other evidence.

As Joseph Beachem turned into the Dartmouth neighborhood, he was struck how normal it appeared. Most of the houses were raised ranches. Some clearly were built in the 1970s, with pitched ornamental overhangs and detailed front doors. It was a quiet neighborhood where yards bumped on three sides and neighbors could easily see who was on the street. The houses were neat and clean, the lawns manicured with bushes trimmed carefully. The neighborhood screamed middle class development and sported street names like Oaklawn and Elmview and Basswood.

This is where it ends, the Saxonburg Chief thought.

Beachem pulled the cruiser as close as possible to the police Incident Command Center trailer and got out. He could see the line of television cameras and reporters to the side. Slowly, the Police Chief and Mayor of Saxonburg, Pennsylvania walked up the driveway of 28 Maplecrest Drive and into the backyard.

He could see the state troopers in the corner of the yard, near a shed. One person was carefully digging. He moved closer. The digging, begun hours earlier, was tedious work. Troopers took turns with a narrow shovel, uncovering the earth inch by inch. Beachem's first thought was it was an archeological dig.

The forensic pathologist, James Pokines, told the troopers shoveling to slow down. He told them could see the soil color was slightly different. They watched as he got onto his knees and with a small hand shovel began to carefully clear away the dirt.

They all dug deeper and saw what looked like a rock. It was a bone. It was a kneecap.

They dug farther, carefully cutting through more tree roots.

Slowly, the hole expanded to roughly four feet.

The skeleton of a man clad in boxer shorts, knees high up, was uncovered in the dirt, intertwined with the roots. He appeared to be slumped over in a seated position.

The dig site was solemn. There was no idle chatter, no dark humor. They were on a mission.

Each time a new bone was found, it was photographed and marked with a laser siting system to create a 3D image of the find. FBI Agent Richard Pires, Massachusetts State Trooper Mike Cherven and others eventually climbed into the four-foot hole to slowly scrape away the dirt. The area circling the remains had been excavated, giving them a small space to crouch.

Each bone found was photographed and catalogued before being placed in a bag. The right femur. The right hand. The left hand. The pelvis. The skull. The lower jaw wasn't attached to the skull. They kept digging carefully, until they found it. It was needed to compare with the dental records of Donald Webb authorities had obtained.

And then the sky turned dark and the rain began to fall, slowly at first, then in torrents. Police had tacked a tarp between the shed and fence to cover the dig as the skeleton – and anything around it—was carefully unearthed. Massachusetts State Police Lt. Brian Canavan ran out to buy a tent, tarps, hammers and nails to expand the coverage over the site. They kept digging, slower now and with a trowel, as more of the remains were uncovered.

Tommy MacDonald began to call retired FBI agents who worked on the case and whose memories helped him finally close it.

Pennsylvania State Police Corporal Chris Birckbichler first called his dad Dale Birckbichler, now long retired from the state police, who made him promise to find the killer of Chief Adams; then District Attorney Richard Goldinger's office in Butler County. Then he called Jim Poydence, the retired Pennsylvania state trooper who started the investigation in 1980 and was vacationing in Canada, followed by a call to the others, including former Chief Gordon Mainhart, the man who struggled to save Adams that fateful December 1980 afternoon. Then he sent text messages to other troopers in Pennsylvania with a single word: Geronimo.

Pennsylvania Trooper Max DeLuca and Massachusetts Trooper David Mackin walked through the attached garage with Lillian Webb as the dig continued in the yard behind them. She paused and looked at him.

"You might want that," she said casually, they would later remember.

DeLuca looked down and saw a plastic green storage tote bin.

"That's the bin I used," she told them, the two recalled.

Mary Ann Jones, Greg Adams' widow, suspected the answer could come today after getting word from the FBI through her lawyer. Not the one she hoped for, not the one she prayed for. But the one that would bring, finally, the horror of December 4, 1980, full circle. It would close a chapter for her family, the town of Saxonburg, Pennsylvania, the law enforcement community.

In the past nearly four decades, she had been down this emotional path several times. There had been the sightings of Greg's killer in the Bahamas, in Florida, in Canada, in Maine, in Massachusetts. There were rumors he was dead, killed by gangsters.

Long ago she compartmentalized what had happened in

1980 in her head and heart. There was the life she had before December 4, 1980, when the world stretched out with wonder and opportunity, when the world was kind and safe, when the world included Greg.

Then there was life after that afternoon, one touched with tears and uncertainty. A widow's world. A world she needed to maneuver as a woman alone with two young boys. A world where she needed to dig into an inner strength she never knew she had. There were two children to raise, a household to run, bills to pay, a life still to live. Through the darkness of grief she knew she needed to find light to survive, to provide the strength to raise children who would only know their father through family stories, photographs, memorials and news clippings. Children who would never recall his voice or see him cheering at their games.

Several years after Greg was killed, she moved out of Saxonburg to a nearby town, creating a slight distance from the pain. Her boys went to school, got jobs, married. Even after remarrying in 1989, she would still pause and think at each of her sons' milestones how Greg should have been standing there. How proud he would have been of his boys. Decades later, she now had a full and beautiful life, with grandchildren and her second husband, splitting her time between winters in Florida and summers in Pennsylvania. But every year, in the weeks leading up to the first week of December, her thoughts yanked her back to that 1980 afternoon. The day the happy-ever-after dream died.

The million-dollar lawsuit against Lillian Webb had been the idea of her youngest son, Greg, and second husband, Jim Jones. It was a sort of "Hail Mary" legal play to convince Webb's wife—officially his ex-wife now—to say where the killer was. Speak up or pay up.

Now, things were moving fast. The fastest since late 1980 and 1981.

First the FBI swooped into the Massachusetts home of Lillian Webb in 2016 and discovered a secret closet-sized room in the basement. Then, the Massachusetts State Police went in months later, seizing the closet door and a cane left behind.

Lillian Webb had stayed silent about where Donald was during both searches, just as she had in the decades earlier. But now, faced with this lawsuit, she promised to talk to authorities. She promised to say where Donald Eugene Webb was.

Special Agent Thomas MacDonald had called to say today might be that day.

Still, Mary Ann wasn't getting her hopes up.

She was sitting at the table in her Florida home when her lawyer, Tom King, called on July 13, 2017.

"Go online," he told her. The local radio station, WBSM-1420, was live streaming from outside Lillian Webb's house.

On her iPad, she watched as a camera, poked through arborvitae trees, caught the shadowy images of police digging. She watched as it panned the street to show police cars lined in front of the home. She watched as the radio station news director, Taylor Cormier, gave his report, saying no one was sure if Webb had been found. She suspected otherwise.

By the end of the night, Mary Ann Jones knew the case was closed.

Donald Webb was likely dead, buried in that backyard.

She had closure but no justice.

Justice would have come at the end of a trial.

"Justice would have been that he would have served time in jail," she later said.

When the call finally came, retired FBI agent Pete McCann wasn't surprised.

Tommy MacDonald gave him a heads up earlier that Webb was likely dead and the fugitive's now ex-wife might finally say where the remains were. Did he want to be there when the killer is unearthed? McCann thought about it for a bit. It would mark the final punctuation in one of the cases that haunted him and his close friend, now-retired Pennsylvania State Police Jim Poydence.

He had been told earlier that no one was quite sure when Webb's former wife would officially talk with investigators or exactly where the killer's remains might be. It was likely in Massachusetts, the retired agent knew, and that was a roughly ten-hour drive from McCann's western Pennsylvania home.

Jim Poydence was out of the country, on vacation with his family. It would be strange to witness the end without one of the people who was there from the start. Besides, he had work lined up with the investigation agency he and Jim set up after they retired.

Instead, on the day of the dig, as young troopers and FBI agents chopped through thick tree roots, Pete McCann sat at home with his wife, Mary, a former FBI employee, and watched the case end on a computer as a radio station live streamed the scene outside the Dartmouth, Massachusetts, house.

George Bates was visiting family in the Mid-Atlantic States with plans to later head up to Massachusetts to see more family and friends when he learned investigators were close to finding the killer's remains.

After decades in the FBI, he was enjoying time in retirement with his family. He thought about accepting the invitation to cut short his time and go to Massachusetts when Webb was dug up. It was a long trip back, both in time and distance, and he had family to visit.

Danny McKnight was working on the computer in his home office, where he ran the Masonic Benefit Trust for the Scottish Rite Valley of New Castle, when he got the call from Chris.

"We got him," Danny was told. Then, the retired trooper called up on his computer the Massachusetts radio website live streaming from the dig site and settled in to watch from afar.

At age 80, Jack McGraw was settled comfortably in a small coastal town in Southeastern Massachusetts. He retired from the FBI in 1993, at the mandatory retirement age of 57, and was now living close to his son, Matt, a local police officer, enjoying good health and a good life. A young agent had stopped by and called several times to talk about Donald Webb over the past couple of years, looking for those bits of information that could, hopefully, finally put the case to rest.

The agent, Thomas MacDonald, was assigned to the Resident Office in Portland, Maine and was interviewing as many of the retired agents, troopers and local cops as he could. The young agent tried to keep him in the loop but Jack knew from his years on the job there were some things he couldn't share. The odds of finding Donald Webb were long and this young agent's work might provide the last chance they had.

Several of the retired agents were told earlier in the week that something might break in the case soon. Soon as in a couple of days.

It was a grey and unseasonably cold summer day and Jack was sitting at home, warm and dry, watching television when the phone rang. It was Tommy MacDonald.

The body of Donald Eugene Webb was found buried in a backyard, he told the retired agent. Did he want to come to the scene?

Jack looked out the window. It was now raining hard. It was cold for July. He was retired. It wasn't his case anymore. Did he really want to go?

He mulled it over for a minute, and at the urging of his wife, went into his bedroom and pulled out fresh clothes: creased pants, a button down shirt, a tie and dress shoes. Proper FBI attire. Then he drove to Dartmouth.

He pulled up to the house, the street lined with police cars, and was ushered by MacDonald to the backyard. He was the only retired FBI agent there. The others were scattered along the East Coast or vacationing with children and grandchildren out-of-state. This day, he knew he was representing all of them and their years of work.

He stayed at the scene for close to three hours under a tent as rain beat hard.

He stayed and looked at the hole near the tree line. The

hole where the man they searched so long and hard for now lay.

"I was glad to be able to live from the beginning to the end," McGraw recalled.

The cold rain pelted reporters clustered outside the Dartmouth house as the investigators dug under the tent. Taylor Cormier from the local radio station WBSM radio was the first reporter there and was still live streaming from the scene. A tipster from town called the station earlier to say there was a lot of police on Maplecrest Drive; a reporter might want to swing by.

Taylor was getting ready to head home when the call came in.

"I'll swing by," he offered.

When he pulled up to Maplecrest Drive 15 minutes later, he knew he would be there for a while.

The street was lined with police vehicles. The one that stood out had Pennsylvania license plates and Saxonburg police on the sides.

WBSM had done several stories earlier about the searches at the house and Cormier was familiar with the Donald Webb case. He wasn't sure what police were doing now but he suspected it was something big.

He could see police in the driveway and people heading into the rear of the house. He looped around the house and asked a neighbor if he could shoot video from that yard. Then, crouched on the porch, he zoomed in through the trees, into the Webb yard. He could see cops digging and wielding what looked like an axe. Another person in blue gloves appeared to be sifting through dirt. He could hear voices. He recognized one: Bristol County District Attorney Thomas Quinn.

He heard someone say they didn't believe Lillian could dig the grave alone.

He called the station, talking with Tim Weisberg, a fellow news anchor and reporter.

Then he began live-streaming the scene on the station's Facebook page, opening a tiny window to the public about what was going on.

Within a half-hour, he was no longer the only reporter there. Within an hour, standing in the rain wearing flip-flops, white shorts, and a cotton shirt with rolled up sleeves, he was soaked. When a station colleague, Chris McCarthy, brought over a rain poncho, his first thought was to keep his camera and phone dry.

From the street and from neighbors' yards, other reporters tried to capture more images of the digging. WPRI-TV Providence cameraman, Johnny Villella, working with reporter Tim White, caught shadowy images of police as they moved in the yard, shoveling dirt.

WFXT Boston 25 reporter Bob Ward and his cameraman, Jackson Stewart, circled the building trying to get a shot of investigators at work, much later getting a shot of the shallow grave. They caught snippets of a person hitting the ground with what appeared to be an axe, someone in blue gloves in the dirt, someone shoveling. The snippets opened a tiny window to the public of what was going on.

No one outside law enforcement knew how extensive—and intricate—the work in the yard was that day.

When investigators search for bodies or bones long buried, it is like an archeological dig. Each layer of dirt carefully examined for disturbances in texture and color. A body changes the dynamics of the soil and its surroundings. The sheer effort of digging then burying someone shifts the dirt, can change the soil color and mixes layers the environment. Leaves and rocks are covered, deep earth exposed.

Investigators first look for depressions on the ground, a sign the earth was disturbed. The second thing may be a change in the color of the grass or brush. When they start to dig, it is a painstaking process. Each shovel of dirt must be sifted for small bones. A bone, over time, can take on the color of the earth. A finger bone resembles a small stick to the untrained eye and easy to miss.

Sometimes an excavator is brought in to help move the earth to start. In Dartmouth, the dig area was cramped. Pick axes, shovels and backbreaking work were required.

Investigators were lucky: they knew where to dig in the Dartmouth yard. But when they are uncertain, dogs trained to find bodies are brought in. Trooper Blackwell's dog, Klaas, was cross trained as a patrol canine and a "cadaver" dog, undergoing the specialized eight-week body hunt training roughly a year and a half earlier.

Cadaver search training for dogs is a specialized field, requiring ongoing work for both handler and canine. Play is often used as a reward for the dogs for a job well done. For Klaas, that meant playing with a tug-toy.

To train a dog to find human remains is a time consuming process. In some cases, a scent material called Pseudo Corpse, or artificial scents such as Cadaverine and Putrescine are used. Other times human blood, flesh, hair and soil samples where human remains had been once found are used, according to *Cadaver Dog Handbook: Forensic Training and Tactics for the Recovery of Human Remains.*

The handbook by Andrew Rebmann, Edward David and Marcella H. Sorg, experts in cadaver dog training, notes the gases, acids and liquids produced in the decaying process are what the dogs are trained to detect. As the body decomposes, different scents are detected. A recently deceased person won't smell as much as one who has been there for a while. The scent also is blended into the soil. Some handlers believe the remains can "feed" into the nearby foliage and trees, spreading that scent.

That is what Tim Blackwell wondered as his dog first barked at the tree, its roots later found woven around the skeleton of Donald Webb the day of the dig. His dog barked, then sat down to signal a find.

By 9:30 that night, Thomas Quinn, the District Attorney for Bristol County, which covers Dartmouth, was standing in the street, across from the house, surrounded by a bevy of reporters. Behind him stood Saxonburg Chief Joseph Beachem and Saxonburg Mayor William Gillespie. To his right, wearing an orange windbreaker, was Massachusetts Assistant Attorney General Patrick Hanley. To his left were Massachusetts State Police Lt. Col. Dermot Quinn and State Police Lt. Michael

Cooney, assigned to the state Attorney General's office.

Tommy MacDonald was way in the back, nearly out of camera range. The rain had finally stopped but the air had an unseasonable nip, harkening to fall. The troopers who did the digging were out of sight.

Tom Quinn was in Fall River earlier that day, getting some work done in the District Attorney's satellite office in the city when he got the call to go to Dartmouth. He was told the day before by one of his prosecutors, Bill McCauley, that police would be digging at Lillian's Dartmouth house and he should be prepared to come by. He grew up in Dartmouth and knew the neighborhood where police were searching—his brother lived two streets away.

The story of Donald Webb was always told with broad strokes—guy from the area killed a cop in another state then disappeared. It wasn't until Tom became the county prosecutor and the FBI reopened the search that he learned the specifics of the case and the extensive efforts to find Webb.

Tom got to the neighborhood around 1:30 that afternoon and parked up the street from the house. The first thing that struck him as he walked to the house were the Arborvitae trees looming high and wide. He was ushered into the yard by State Police and gazed at the work site. Teams of police officers, some digging, some sifting dirt. Some of the people he knew. There was Trooper Tim Blackwell and his K9 Klaas, a five-year-old Belgian Malinois. There was Crime Scene specialist Trooper David Mackin and firearms identification specialist Trooper Nuno Medeiros. He spotted troopers assigned to the Attorney General's office—a few once worked in his office, such as Mike Cherven. Tom talked a bit with the State Police Colonel Dermot Quinn, no relation, and his own two prosecutors at the scene, McCauley and Patrick Blomberg to get what he called a "lay of the land."

After about an hour, Quinn left for his main office in New Bedford to check on the ongoing cases in the county then returned later in the day. It was raining hard late in the afternoon when he returned. Quinn remembered thinking he really should have brought an umbrella.

By nightfall, the group of reporters outside the house had grown. There were live trucks parked along the street. Television crews from Boston and Rhode Island were there. So were reporters from radio stations and newspapers. Some wore rain slickers. Many did not. It was bleak, dark and cold. It was time to release some information to the press.

With the television cameras trained on him, the District Attorney addressed the group.

"Good evening everybody," the prosecutor told the reporters. "State troopers assigned to the Massachusetts Attorney General's Office of Maura Healey obtained a search warrant for 28 Maplecrest Drive, the address across the street.

"That search warrant was executed today. It was related to the murder of Chief Gregory Adams of Saxonburg, Pennsylvania on December 4th, 1980. As a result of the execution of the search warrant, what appeared to be human remains have been discovered. An autopsy will be conducted and an identification of the remains will be attempted during that process which will occur shortly.

"I want to thank the Attorney General's Office in Massachusetts, Maura Healey, and their troopers for initiating this portion of the investigation, again relating to the death of Chief Adams," he said.

He then thanked the FBI, the Pennsylvania State Police, the state police assigned to his office. "The investigation is ongoing. As I said, it will continue. At this point, there is not much more I can say," he told the reporters.

"I also would like to acknowledge Chief Joe Beachem here from Saxonburg Police Department who is present here today. I would like to thank them for taking the time to come down here for a matter that is part of the investigation that is important to them. At this point, that is all I have. I will take a couple of questions if I can but I'm not going to get into too many specifics."

One reporter asked where the body was buried. Another asked how long the body was there. Yet another asked if anyone would be charged. The District Attorney was cautious in his answers.

The body was found in the backyard, in the left area of the property, he told them.

He wouldn't comment on how long the body was there —or confirm that it was that of Donald Webb. A warrant had been issued for Webb, he noted. A forensic examination would be conducted.

"What appeared to be human remains were recovered," was the only concrete piece of information he would release.

Technically, the case fell under the jurisdiction of the District Attorney's Office in Bristol County as an "unattended death" but the investigation that lead everyone there rested in the hands of the FBI, Pennsylvania State Police and Massachusetts state troopers assigned to the Attorney General's Office. It would be up to those other agencies in the next hours and days to provide the details on what lead to the discovery. For now, the basic news seemed to be enough: it appeared the killer was found.

Soon after the press conference, the dig was over. The tent shielding the makeshift grave was packed up. The skeletal remains were en route to the Medical Examiner's Office in Boston to be officially identified. The gun found buried in the dirt was bagged as evidence. The man accused of killing a police chief with a young family, who eluded authorities for decades, was finally found.

The investigators from three agencies, some children at the time of the killing, drove from the Dartmouth house which had been the focus of their attention for so long to a chain restaurant to get something to eat not far from the Massachusetts State Police barracks off Interstate 195.

Inside, one person placed a photograph of Chief Gregory Adams on the bar, facing them.

They raised a glass in his memory.

They raised a glass to finding a killer.

Chapter 10
Justice

Gordon Mainhart listened to the radio as he waited in the parking lot in his 2011 Subaru Outback while his wife wrapped up a hairdressing appointment. On the back of his SUV were two emblems: one in memory of Chief Adams and one of the Marine Corp. He was trying not to think about Greg and that December 1980 afternoon. Being in the back of the ambulance, pleading with Greg to hang on. But the memories first tickled the corners of his mind then washed over in waves. He was back in the ambulance, racing to the hospital. He could hear himself saying, hang on, hang on. He could remember the hope Greg would.

It was the day after police unearthed the skeletal remains in a Dartmouth, Massachusetts, backyard. Mainhart knew it was likely those of the long sought killer. He knew some of the details of what happened. The suspect's wife told state police in general terms what happened after the killing, where Webb hid, how he hid, how he died. She told them how she buried him in her backyard.

But after years of false leads and false hopes, Gordon felt doubt tugging at his soul. What, he wondered, if it wasn't Webb in that makeshift grave? What if this decades long search wasn't over? As he waited outside the Winfield Road hair salon for his wife, Terry, he worried. There had been too many times since December 4, 1980, when they all held false hopes, so many times when it appeared Webb was within their grasp. So many times he wasn't.

Gordon wanted to be in Dartmouth to witness the dig, to see firsthand the killer's body—or bones. But there had been some logistical law enforcement travel conflicts that prevented him from going, leaving Gordon home, waiting and hoping to hear it was finally over.

So, he sat there in his SUV, waiting for his wife, biding time.

Then his LG flip phone sounded at 12:06 p.m. It was a text message from Pennsylvania State Police Corporal Chris Birckbichler. There were just two words:

POSITIVE ID!

His eyes burned with tears. He felt a chill through his body.

Chris Birckbichler and Max DeLuca were quiet as they waited for the Pennsylvania State Police plane to land at New Bedford Municipal Airport to bring them home to Pennsylvania. It had been two days since the bones of Donald Eugene Webb were dug up in his wife's backyard, and one day since those remains were positively identified as that of the accused killer of Saxonburg Police Chief Gregory Adams. The small airport was at the end of an industrial park, nestled near a cemetery, highway, and homes in the north end of New Bedford, where, on average, half-dozen flights took off daily in July of 2017.

The state police Cessna was set to land shortly and the two Pennsylvania investigators were thinking about the Saxonburg Chief, closure and what justice means.

On Christmas Eve 1980, the name and description of Donald Eugene Webb, aka Donald Perkins, aka Stanley J. Portas, aka S. John Portas, was entered into the National Crime Information Center from the Butler State Police barracks and sent out on teletype to police departments across the country. Now, 36 years later, Chris Birckbichler was calling the State Police dispatcher, Becky Darney, at the barracks on his cellphone.

He put the call on speaker so Max could hear.

"Becky, I need you to run a name," Chris told her. "Donald Eugene Webb."

He paused as she pulled the name up on the computer. She confirmed it was an active entry.

"Please, take that out of NCIC," he said.

He could hear her typing on the other end.

"Could you please print out a copy for me and please print out a copy for Max."

Law enforcement agents throughout the country—many who were children or not even born when Chief Adams was killed—would now know Donald Eugene Webb, date of birth July 14, 1931, wanted on charges of murder, on the FBI Most Wanted list for decades, was now officially found.

As the plane took flight that bright, sunny day, Chris Birckbichler stared out the airplane window. It was quiet and he could feel a surge of satisfaction. It was over.

The day after Webb's remains were unearthed, retired Rhode Island State Police detective Lt. Tommy Denniston said he was at Rhode Island State Police Headquarters, meeting with three high-ranking members of the department. Several retired law enforcement officials said Denniston, when he was on the job, was respected for his work. But things were different now that he was no longer on the department.

Some people were saying Denniston was working with the well-known defense attorney known for representing mobsters and were suspect of his motives in contacting different investigators. Denniston, in a later interview, said that surprised him. He said he still was concerned the FBI didn't do all it could in the early days to find the fugitive and wondered if that was because Webb was an informant, like the notorious Whitey Bulger, but believed these new federal investigators did a great job in resolving the case. He said he just wanted to learn why Webb hadn't been found earlier. He wasn't working for the defense or Lillian Webb or her son, he insisted. He said the first time he met Lillian was the day Webb's remains were unearthed.

At the meeting at Rhode Island State Police Headquarters, Denniston asked if his source could get the reward in the Webb case. The person could also obtain information about another unsolved crime, he said.

The answer was simple: the source—who Denniston wouldn't identify to law enforcement—wasn't entitled to the reward. No follow up meeting was scheduled.

At the courthouse office in Saxonburg, Judge Sue Haggerty pulled a file out of the cabinet. For decades, the arrest warrant for Donald Eugene Webb, Docket No. C-283-80, was kept in the drawer. It was there when Judge James H. Galbreath signed it, back when she was an administrative assistant for the court, and it was there now, nearly four decades later.

She was now the judge in the Saxonburg court, making sure the paperwork for this case had made the move to the new courtroom offices a block away from the old one in the municipal building. She made sure it was never misplaced, always ready to be served once the accused killer was found.

She was the person now who would mark the court case against Donald Eugene Webb closed.

Chapter 11
Returning To Saxonburg

By the time Saxonburg Police Chief Joseph Beachem and Mayor William Gillespie left the dig site, it was rainy and dark and cold for a July night. They opted not to join the investigators for dinner, planning instead to get a quick bite to eat and spend the night in New Bedford at the Marriot overlooking the city's working waterfront before heading out early the next day. Neither man had been in this part of New England before. They could see the history as they walked along cobblestone streets—a whaling museum, the Seamen's Bethel featured in the 1956 film Moby Dick featuring Gregory Peck, the U.S. Customhouse built in 1836.

It had been a long and emotional ride to Massachusetts. For 37 years, people in Saxonburg honored the memory of the Chief on the anniversary of his death while investigators traveled the country, following up tips. Greg Adams was never forgotten. But there was always an unsettledness mixed with the memory. People developed theories to try to find logic to the murder and how Webb escaped capture. Did someone in the area hide Webb? Did a local doctor with reputed mob ties treat him? Was the Chief targeted because of the drug work he did in Washington, D.C.?

Now, after years of questions, there was an answer. Two strangers—one a lawman, one a crook—met in a brief, fatal encounter in a quiet town on a quiet street just weeks before

Christmas. The Chief battled for his life, kicking and clawing, leaving lifelong injuries on the man he never knew. He fought when the gun went off. He fought as he lay dying of gunshot wounds. He fought to get home, to return to his family.

The killer who seemed to vanish, the man dubbed The Ghost, lived a lifetime of pain. He wasn't shot but his injuries would haunt his daily existence. The pain never left. Authorities now knew the bones found curled in the dirt behind the ranch-style house on Maplecrest Drive in Dartmouth, Massachusetts were likely those of Donald Eugene Webb. A comparison of dental records and DNA, as early as the next day, would provide the official confirmation. But they knew— everyone who was in that backyard watching the digging knew—the skeleton clad in a T-shirt, boxer shorts and covered with an empty bag of lime was that of the long-sought killer.

The search was over.

The Chief and Mayor planned to leave by nine the next morning for Saxonburg. It was the kickoff for a weekend-long celebration and they needed to be there: the 185th anniversary of the town's founding by John Roebling and the 175th anniversary of Roebling's patent for the new wire twisting technique that eventually made creation of the Brooklyn Bridge possible. It was a big deal for the town. The great-great-great-grandson of John Roebling, Kriss Roebling, would be on hand for the two-day celebration July 15 and 16.

Fred Caesar, curator of the town's Saxonburg Museum, invited the direct descendent of the founder to attend and was pleasantly surprised when the man said yes. This would be the first time a Roebling would be in town in more than 30 years and only two other descendants had visited in the previous 135 years (and then almost 30 years apart) since the founder packed up his business in 1849 and moved to Trenton, New Jersey.

This visit was pretty exciting.

Kriss Roebling would first walk in the parade with his family July 15. He would place flowers on the grave of the only two some family members buried in the Saxonburg Memorial Church Cemetery. He would attend Sunday services the next day in the original church building his great-great-great grandfather built in 1837 and maintained by Saxonburg Memorial Presbyterian Church. That same Sunday, on July 16, he would tour the workshop where his great-great-great-grandfather did early work on the wire rope process used on the Brooklyn Bridge. He would be standing in the workshop 175 years to the day when U.S. Patent 2720 for the process was received.

It was to be a magnificent celebration.

Fred Caesar spent the days and weeks and months leading up to the July 15-16 double anniversary with a group of residents planning and organizing. It would be an exciting time for the town that loved to celebrate. And there were plenty of family-friendly celebrations in Saxonburg. There was the Main Street Mingles, started by the late Mayor Pam Bauman, featuring once a year the "Mayor's Table" consisting of banquet tables stretched along Main Street with food from local restaurants and food trucks. There was the Pet Parade featuring snakes, camels, cats, dogs and other animals. There was the Fireman's Parade, drawing fire companies throughout the region. There was the Saxonburg Volunteer Fireman's Carnival. Chief Beachem once joked the town loved community celebrations so much it would hold a parade for a parade.

So when Chief Beachem and Mayor Gillespie hit the road the day after Webb was dug up, they knew there would be no downtime once they got home. Saxonburg would be in a full historic celebratory mode. They weren't sure how many knew there was another reason to cheer.

They were about two hours out on the road when Massachusetts State Police Sgt. Kevin Baker called.

The Medical Examiner confirmed what they suspected. The man buried behind the house was Donald Eugene Webb.

Linda Kovacik, the police department's part-time administrative assistant, fielded call after call to the Saxonburg Police Department. One was from the *Boston Globe* newspaper. Another from the *Pittsburgh Post-Gazette*. Another from WPRI, the CBS affiliate in Providence, Rhode Island. There were likely more calls taken by administrative assistants in the borough offices upstairs while she was on the phone. All of the reporters wanted one thing: to confirm the body of Chief Adams' killer had been found.

Earlier that day, Chief Beachem called to say he was in Massachusetts with the Mayor and it appeared the man who shot Chief Adams in 1980 was found dead. It was information for her ears only. "Don't tell anyone where we are or what is going on," he cautioned her. Someone from the FBI called soon after to say the same thing.

Linda knew the importance of being discreet. As the secretary/treasurer for 23 years with the Saxonburg borough, she knew what information she could release and what she could not. Someone once told her a secretary was someone who knew when to keep her mouth shut when dealing with sensitive material. She was now working part-time at the police department as its first police clerk, her new post-retirement job, where that type of discretion was key.

"You need to talk with the Chief," she told each of the callers.

And as each asked to be transferred to his office, she politely noted he wasn't in at the time. She didn't say where he was. She didn't say when he would return. She didn't let on that she knew he was in Massachusetts. She simply logged the names of the media outlets and the time of the calls.

When she looked up from her desk near the front counter between calls, she could see the police department lobby through the Plexiglas window. She could see the framed citations and photographs along the walls honoring Chief Gregory Adams, a man she never met but whose legacy she knew.

Saxonburg Officer Beau Sneddon strolled through downtown as the town's dual anniversary festivities started. The road was blocked from the Memorial Church at the top of West Main Street to the Municipal building and the people milling along the closed street kept stopping to shake his hand.

"Congratulations," one man said.

"Great job," said another.

"What can you tell us?" asked yet another person.

Beau smiled and nodded and told each person the same thing when they asked for more information: "Not much more I can tell you."

And there wasn't. Beau and his brother, Jeff Sneddon, who worked as an officer for the nearby Buffalo Township police department, were close friends with Chief Beachem and talked daily. They thought it strange when cruiser 345, the Chief's car, was gone from the police lot earlier in the week and called him.

"I can't tell you right now," Beachem told him. "When I can I will. "

Beau thought his boss was working a drug case or robbery case in the area. Confidential stuff that couldn't, or shouldn't, be shared. Finding the man who killed Chief Greg Adams in 1980 didn't cross his mind.

When Beachem did call later it was from the backyard of a Dartmouth, Massachusetts home. He told Beau that the man they had been hunting for decades had been hiding in a home in Massachusetts.

"They are digging him up," the Chief told him.

"What do you mean, they're digging him up?" Beau asked.

"I'll tell you later."

By Saturday morning, the kick off day for the town anniversary celebration, just about everyone in town got word the killer was found dead and buried. It was, some said, as if the sun finally burned off the dark clouds of grief hovering over Saxonburg.

The Mayor and Chief Beachem were treated as heroes when they got back to town. Just about everyone wanted to talk. Everyone wanted to slap them on the back, shake their hands, say thank you. And each time, the pair would credit the state police in Massachusetts and Pennsylvania and FBI Special Agent Thomas MacDonald who helped pull the case to its end.

Fred Caesar, the curator of the Saxonburg Museum, watched from the announcer's parade platform on Main Street July 15, 2017 as hundreds lined the street, celebrating both the town and the news that the killer of Greg Adams was finally found. Saxonburg police cruiser 345 was at the head of the nineteen-minute parade.

Police Officer Beau Sneddon, behind the wheel, stopped as the four man group—comprised of Jim Knapick, Bob Norris, David Brooks and Ron Brooks—sang a moving rendition of the Star Spangled Banner as townspeople stood at attention, hands over their hearts. Fred Caesar watched as the Knoch High School Knights baton twirlers, cheerleaders and marching band performed.

As the classic Ford Model T truck drove 99-year-old Alfred C. Maurhoff, a descendent of one of the families that came to Saxonburg in 1833, waved to the crowd, a blanket over his legs.

There were John Deere tractors from the local Agway, fire trucks honking, ambulances sounding the occasional alarm.

There was the 1967 Jeep with a cow, kayak, bicycle and large grasshopper used by the Butler County tourism to promote the area.

There were Girl Scouts and trucks and business sponsored cars.

There was the 1926 Model T Ford owned by the local Neubert family and the 1939 American Bantam car made in Butler County owned by the Butler County Tourism and Convention Bureau.

The parade ended with the same car that kicked it off.

Saxonburg Police Department cruiser 345.

The same police cruiser parked outside the Dartmouth, Massachusetts, home as the remains of killer Donald Eugene Webb were dug up.

It was, Fred Caesar knew, as the television stations from

nearby Pittsburgh began arriving to get town reaction to the discovery, a great day for Saxonburg.

A week after the remains of Webb were identified, Tommy MacDonald and Rich Pires called the aging mobster who once ran with Webb in a different era. Rich kept in touch with Frank Lach after those first Florida visits, once stopping by the assisted living/nursing facility to say hello while on vacation with his family. "I was just checking in. He was very happy to see me again. I brought him some type of a sub, it was a meatball sub or something like that and he and I chatted for a half an hour … One of the suggestions we had for him was to write everything he knew in a letter and put it in a safe deposit box. He considered it and said 'there are people out there who are still alive that I can't betray."

The FBI agents were calling Lach to let him know Webb was found.

"He was excited to hear from us," Rich said. "We told him, 'Hey, Frank, we got him.'"

"Hey boys, nice work," Lach answered, Rich and Tommy recalled.

It was one day before the close of National Police Week and Ben Adams was looking out from the gazebo podium, preparing to speak.

It was nearly a year since the man who killed his father was found and more than two dozen people were gathered in the park yards from the museum honoring the town's founder. The stretch of Butler Street where his father fought for his life was a few blocks away. It would be renamed today—May 18, 2018—as Gregory B. Adams Way.

The former Mayor, Jody Pfluegler, said the installation of the new street sign would serve as a reminder of the sacrifices law enforcement officers make daily.

Gordon Mainhart, the man who was with the Chief the last minutes of his life that 1980 afternoon, clutched a slip of paper with a short handwritten speech and thanked the investigators for finding the killer. "To all of us left, especially Mary Ann and the boys, may God bless and take care. I believe Greg, Chief Adams, is still watching over us all."

Joseph Beachem, the current Chief, told of what the community lost in the weeks before Christmas of 1980.

He said, "The family of Chief Adams has long suffered from the loss of a husband and father. The residents of Saxonburg have grieved the loss of an honorable officer. Retired Chief Mainhart, who was with Chief Adams in the ambulance that fateful December day in 1980 lost a mentor and a friend. The world, by all accounts, lost a good man.

"The signs designating this section of road, will stand as a reminder that a good man did great things for his community. This will remind us, as his successors in law enforcement, that evil can rear its ugly head anywhere, at any time. These signs will stand as tribute to his sacrifice and ensure that we are reminded to be vigilant. Above all, his name will be displayed for all passing by to see, to know, and remember that a brave man doing brave things one horrible December afternoon, paid the ultimate price."

Ben listened as the current Chief quoted the first century Roman historian and senator, Tacitus, who would solemnly greet visitors with the words, "In valor, there is hope."

"Chief Adams' confrontation with evil exemplified valor," the current Chief told the group.

The Mayor, William Gillespie, told those gathered to remember Chief Adams for his commitment to the community, for his love of family, for his sacrifice.

"The memory of Chief Adams and the sacrifice he made will never be forgotten and we pledge to uphold the standards of police service he established here," Gillespie said.

Speakers praised the work of FBI Special Agent Thomas MacDonald, Pennsylvania State Police Corporal Chris Birckbichler and Trooper Max DeLuca, Massachusetts State Police Sgt. Kevin Baker and Massachusetts trooper Mike Cherven. They praised the work of the investigators now retired and those who took up the cause over the decades. The list, they would later say, was long.

Ben Adams eventually stood at the podium, the family's representative for this dedication, to address the group. His younger brother, Greg, married with children, lived in Florida. His mother wasn't expected back in Pennsylvania from Florida, where she spent the winters near her grandchildren, until the next day.

He talked about his father—a man killed when he was a toddler, who existed in a memory of phantom images. A man who went out to work one day and never came back.

He thanked the community for never forgetting, the FBI agents and Pennsylvania and Massachusetts State Police investigators who never gave up.

"My father fought and died doing everything he possibly could to find his way home," Ben told the audience. "And that is dedication. And that is the thing people need to remember—those people who go out every single day to dedicate their lives for the public good in every way. That is my father's legacy. "

The audience sat in silence as he continued.

"Sadly, my family my mother, my brother, my two nieces, my nephew, they may never know true justice … However, we do have closure and a resolution to the case thanks to the dedication of the Pennsylvania State Police, the Federal Bureau of Investigation and the Massachusetts State Police state police," he said, crediting current and retired law enforcement members who "dedicated so much time and energy and never gave up on this case."

As the National Police Week neared a close, as people across the country remembered officers killed in the line of duty, the group gathered around the gazebo in Saxonburg paused in prayer.

"We thank you for your service, Chief Adams," The Rev. Douglas M. Dorsey, senior pastor at Saxonburg Memorial Presbyterian Church, said.

Epilogue

More than a year after the bones of Donald Eugene Webb were unearthed, the members of Retired Pennsylvania State Police Association of Pennsylvania gathered for its 63rd annual banquet at the Marriott North in Cranberry Township, about a dozen miles from Saxonburg.

On the menu this September 2018 night were grilled salmon, stuffed chicken breast, vegetarian Mediterranean purse, mile-high apple pie with caramel, some laughs and a few war stories.

Danny R. McKnight, the association's outgoing president, looked across the room, seeing the faces of the men he once worked with. They were all much older now, many with less hair and more waist. But he—and the others in the room—could remember the youthful energy they all shared patrolling roads, investigating cases, finding answers.

The spotlight would be on that energy tonight—and on answers found.

At the head table with McKnight were Chris Birckbichler; the incoming association president Eric Reese; Arlene Mulholland, president of the Ladies Auxiliary; Dan Fiscus, secretary/treasurer of the retirees association; Jonathon Lindsay, a representative of the Pennsylvania State Troopers Association; and Capt. Steve Ignatz, commander of the Butler Barracks along with their spouses.

Sitting at tables nearby in the banquet room were Mary Ann Jones, Gordon Mainhart, James Poydence, Pete McCann, retired trooper Al Vish and the former administrative assistant Sue Haggerty, who was now a district judge.

The guest speaker for the night, sitting at that head table, was FBI Special Agent Thomas MacDonald.

It marked the first time many of the Pennsylvania State Police investigators who opened the murder case in 1980 would meet the FBI agent who helped close it.

Tommy MacDonald was looking forward to this night, where he could shake the hands of the troopers, some now in their 70s and 80s who worked 24/7 in those early months, whose documented work helped him nearly 40 years later. There had been an earlier gathering in 2017 with current and retired Massachusetts investigators, a few weeks after the killer's remains were found, at a Middleboro, Massachusetts, restaurant. At that luncheon, retired troopers like Dan Lowney and retired FBI agent Jack McGraw were there to hear Tommy explain how Webb was found. There was a shared sense of euphoria and success in the room that day.

Massachusetts was where the case ended.

Here in Pennsylvania, though, is where it started.

Earlier in the day, Tommy went to Saxonburg with Pennsylvania State Police Corporal Chris Birckbichler to present the Police Chief with a framed FBI Ten Most Wanted Fugitive poster with "RESOLVED" stamped across Webb's photo. He also gifted the department with a specialized Axis baseball bat made in Fall River, Massachusetts, the stomping grounds of Webb's old gang. The bat was painted Steelers black and gold. The Pennsylvania State Police logo was on one end, the Massachusetts State police logo on the other. In the center was the FBI insignia.

At the Saxonburg Police Department where plaques and citations honoring Chief Greg Adams line the narrow lobby, the slain man's son, Ben, said a few words. Tommy finally met the last person to see Greg Adams alive: Gordon Mainhart, the other full-time officer on the two-man department who road with the dying Adams in the ambulance.

Hours later, at the retirees banquet, Tommy would meet many of the men who he knew only from hours-long tele-

phone calls. The men who were there from the start. Jim Poydence, Al Vish, Danny McKnight, from the Pennsylvania State
Police and Pete McCann who worked in the FBI Pennsylvania
offices. Tommy would meet others touched by the case such
as Nancy Bard, a nurse who was in the emergency room the
afternoon the Chief was brought into the hospital.

He would ask everyone who knew Greg Adams or who
worked on the case to rise. Then people at table after table
stood solemnly.

Danny McKnight, who was also a chaplain, gave the
benediction before the meal.

"Almighty God, most merciful Father, we pray that our
Brother Officers who have given their all, in protecting the
lives and properties of American citizens, will be blessed with
Thy favor and everlasting peace. We pray You will render
compassion and understanding to their families and friends
who mourn their departure from this life. Lift up their hearts
and remove all bitterness from their minds knowing a far better life of heavenly bliss awaits them in the eternal home of all
Saints, for this we beg for the honor of His name to whom we
give glory both now and forevermore. AMEN."

Tommy, the keynote speaker, then talked about the case
before presenting investigators with the same type of baseball
bat he gave to the Saxonburg Department.

During dinner, Chris Birckbichler, who was age 13 when
the Chief was killed, looked around the room. He could see
the past meet the present at each table. Retired and current
troopers. Retired and current FBI agents. Friends and family.
All smiling.

Gordon Mainhart was beaming as he slapped Tommy on
the back. It was one of the first times Birckbichler could remember seeing Gordon so gleeful.

Mary Ann Jones, Chief Adams' widow, recounted to
Chris how for years she would get depressed after Thanksgiv-
ing, a darkness lifting only after the holidays. In 2017, the year
Webb was finally found, that the shadow was gone.

She would often say after the bones were found that there
was no justice for her first husband or his family. Webb never

went to trial on murder charges. He never faced a judge or a jury who would decide his fate. Instead, he lived out his life, spent time with his wife, had steak dinners, watched television. He lived with the injuries the Chief inflicted on him that December 4, 1980, afternoon. He lived with some pain. He lived in secret, always looking over his shoulder. But he lived.

There was no justice, she said, but there was finally closure.

As Chris looked around the room that night, he saw the lives Greg Adams touched both in life and in death.

"You hear about a story like this or you read it in a newspaper," he remembers telling the FBI agent's wife that night. "When you do, it is a one-dimensional story.

"This is not a story. This is life."

Acknowledgements, End Notes, and Bibliography

When the remains of Donald Eugene Webb were unearthed on a cold, rainy July day, I wondered: how could someone hide so easily for so long in a city I once covered as a police reporter for more than a decade?

I started work as a police reporter in the New Bedford, Massachusetts fishing port four years after Chief Gregory Adams was killed. Some people occasionally talked about his stepson who had left the police department. No one was talking about Donald Webb. I didn't even know he was still a fugitive. Neither did many local cops over the decades.

This story is one of the community of Saxonburg that never forgot, teams of investigators that never gave up and the family of Chief Gregory Adams who still live with the loss. I am very grateful to everyone who helped me tell this story, especially the last law enforcement team that brought it to a close: Tommy MacDonald, Chris Birckbichler, Max DeLuca and Mike Cherven. They epitomize what can be done when agencies work together.

From the moment my husband and I first drove into Saxonburg in 2018 as part of this project, we knew we found a special place. Thank you to everyone in Saxonburg who opened up your hearts and shared memories. We are in debt to Joseph Beachem who showed us around the community and Gordon

Mainhart, Sue Haggerty and Glenn Fair who proved Saxonburg shines.

There are many who quietly helped behind the scenes in the research of this book. Special thanks to Margaret Hewitt, special collections librarian at the Butler Public Library who helped find archival photos, Kathy Bollinger at the Tarentum branch of the community Library of Allegheny Valley who found the yearbook photo of Chief Adams, Patricia McPherson at the Stonehill College Library as well the library staff at the Fall River Public Library, the New Bedford Public Library and the Taunton Public Library in Massachusetts. Fred Caesar, curator at the Saxonburg Museum, offered invaluable insight into the history of Saxonburg and provided historic context to why the community is so special. Public libraries and community museums are essential to a community. Please support them.

A special shout out to the staffs at local newspapers in Pennsylvania, past and current. The documentation of the case in the early days by the *Butler Eagle* and the *Valley News* preserved the shock of the community, the horror of the killing and the determination of everyone to solve this case. It was a difficult story to report and write but they excelled.

Thank you also to the editors of the *Herald News* of Fall River, the *Standard-Times* of New Bedford and *The Taunton Daily Gazette* for their patience, friendship and assistance. Also, special thanks to Curt Brown, a longtime reporter at both the Fall River and New Bedford newspapers, for his early help and sharing his respected insights into the Fall River gang.

The staff of WBSM radio, and its reporting of the case, as well as the work of local television icons, Bob Ward from Boston 25, and Tim White from WPRI-12 in Providence, Rhode Island, helped provide context to the excavation of the remains in 2017.

Also, a hat tip to long-time WBSM talk show host Philip Paleologos and his wife, Celeste, the former owners of a New Bedford diner, who graciously shared their time as this book was pieced together. Journalism matters and local journalism is part of the fabric of our lives. Support it. Subscribe. The reporters who bring you the news are your neighbors. Keep reading and listening to their reports.

There are a number of people whose help was invaluable. They include Kristen Setera and her colleagues in the FBI Public Affairs Office in Boston; Emalie Gainey in Massachusetts Attorney General Maura Healey's Public Affairs Office; David Procopio from the Massachusetts State Police Public Affairs Office; and Gregg Miliotte from the Bristol County District Attorney's Office. Retired Massachusetts State Police Lt. Kenneth Martin and Lt. Richard Lauria provided advice on the intricacies of crime scenes and its history.

We should all be grateful for the hard work of the FBI agents and members of Pennsylvania State Police and Massachusetts State Police, both retired and current, who never gave up in the hunt for a killer. Daniel Lowney, who has since passed away, was a remarkable investigator whose skills are still talked about to this day.

I am eternally grateful to Special Agents Thomas MacDonald, Phil Torsney and Noreen Gleason for the time and care they took as I researched this book.

Also, retired agent George Bates never lost patience as I kept calling, emailing and texting to double check information about what happened in Massachusetts. Retired Pennsylvania James Poydence and retired Special Agent Pete McCann never gave up and their meticulous notes (and fantastic memories) from that time were critical for this book and the investigation leading to the killer's discovery. Both were on my speed dial.

Also, a shout out to Danny McKnight and John Crede whose work on the case helped keep it in the spotlight.

Retired New Bedford police officers Gardner Greany, Richard Ferreira, James Sylvia, Paul Boudreau, retired Deputy Chief Antero Gonsalves shared their insights about police work in the 1980s in New Bedford. Also, Kenneth Martin and Richard Lauria for making sure the crime scene information was accurate.

Others who helped behind the scenes, whether by taking my calls, sitting to talk or providing insight to the case and time included Bob Hargraves, Bruce Gordon, Bob Jones, Robert St. Jean, Chris Ballina, Jack O'Neill, Louis Pacheco, Bruce Gordon, Bob Jones, Chris Ballina, Joe Costa, Jim Watson, Jack O'Neill, Phil Warish, Raymond Veary, Addison Steiner, Paul Walsh Jr., Nelson Offringa, Jose Gonsalves, Preston Paull and Mary Ann Dill.

Frank Lach died in Florida in 2017 after a period of failing health, four months after Donald Webb's remains were found. His sister, MaryAnne DeBalsi, who would visit him in Florida, brought him back to Rhode Island where he is buried in a family plot. She said she saw a different side of her brother: one who was kind, funny and attentive. He didn't talk about his other life.

The list of those who worked on this case is long and most are included in this book. My sincere apologies in advance to those I may have missed.

The strength of Mary Ann Adams Jones, the Chief's widow, and her willingness to relive that painful time still amazes me. She survived an unfathomable loss and I am so grateful she shared her memories with me. She never found justice for her husband but she did find some answers. I don't know if that is enough.

The feedback by early readers Mary Ann Dill, Nancy Harding, Elaine McArdle and my husband, Kevin Kalunian, was invaluable. The support from my husband and son Christian was crucial when I was holed up in my office. An extra thank you to friend and author Elaine McArdle who kept me writing and whose insights were invaluable. Her encouragement when I hit dead ends and her suggestions on the manuscript, while working on her own book, kept me from giving up.

Repeated efforts were made to interview the killer's wife and his stepson by phone, through their attorneys and by mail. Lillian Webb never answered the note slipped under her front door and later declined to be interviewed, through a message from her attorney's office. Her son did not respond to a number of interview requests, including messages left at his business. All direct quotes attributed to Lillian Webb are from an interview with law enforcement the day of the dig. Other quotes are attributed to law enforcement officers' recollections.

There are many unanswered questions about how Donald Webb was able to escape detection for decades. It appears he may have taken some of those answers to the grave.

End Notes

Chapter 1
The Killing

The description of the initial discovery of the fatally wounded Chief Greg Adams by the Freehling family and quotes came from the author's interview with Donald Freehling and December 1980 articles in *The Butler Eagle*, the *Valley News Dispatch*, the *Pittsburgh Post Gazette* and the *Associated Press* as well as information from investigators' notes.

The news stories included:

" 'Pray for me,' cries dying officer," by the Associated Press, Dec. 6, 1980

"Killer of Saxonburg Chief sought," by Kay Walkup, Butler (PA) Eagle, Dec. 5, 1980

"Policeman slain in Saxonburg" by Tony Klimko, Valley News (PA) Dispatch

"Saxonburg Police Chief slain in lot by motorist," by Thomas J. Porter Jr. and Chet Wade, Post Gazette (Pittsburgh, PA), Dec. 5, 1980

Quotes and information about the discovery of the wounded Chief Gregory B. Adams after police were called, the ride to the hospital, and the response to the scene in Saxonburg came from interviews by the author with Brian Antoszyk, Glenn Fair, Donald Freehling, Gordon Mainhart, and Sue Haggerty, James Poydence, John Crede, Dale Birckbichler, Danny McKnight, Pete McCann, Francis Rhyshek and Sue Haggerty. All quotes are based on the recollections of the individuals interviewed and were reviewed with them for accuracy.

Quotes and information in the scene at the Adams home came from author interviews with Mary Ann Adams Jones and her sister, Alida Yoezle, and reflect their recollections of what was said and were reviewed for accuracy.

Information about the funeral of Chief Adams came from news articles and author interviews with people who had been there or were familiar with the situation. Those interviewed included Gordon Mainhart, Mary Ann Jones, Robert Paroli, Robert and James Poydence.

A number of newspaper articles were also used as references, including:

"Slain Chief Had 'Special Call,' Cabot Priest Says." By Kris B. Manula, Butler(PA) Eagle, December 8, 1980.

"500 officers pay tribute to comrade." By Pat Vido, Valley News (PA) Dispatch, December 8, 1980.

"450 policemen line Saxonburg street to pay respects," by Chet Wade, Pittsburgh Post-Gazette, December 8, 1980.

"Killer of Saxonburg Chief sought," by Kay Walkup, Butler Eagle, December 5, 1980.

"Long Blue Line of Officers Pay Tribute to Chief," by Kay Walkup, Butler Eagle, December 8, 1980.

"Police Need Break to Nab Chief's Killer," by Kay Walkup, Butler Eagle, September 22, 1981.

The Teletype message came from Gordon Mainhart's personal archives.

Chapter 2
The Search

Information about the search in Pennsylvania, New Jersey and Massachusetts came from author interviews with Jim Poydence, who relied on his extensive personal notes and records from that time. Also, additional author interviews with George Bates, John Crede, Pete McCann, Paul Fitzgerald, Bruce

Gordon, Patrick Hunt, Daniel Lowney and Sue Haggerty were used.

Background about Donald and Lillian Webb came from public records in New Bedford and Dartmouth, Massachusetts, police reports from Colonie, New York, archival newspaper articles and author interviews with George Bates, Jim Poydence, Pete McCann and Paul Boudreau.

Information about the discovery of the rental car came from author interviews with John Crede, George Bates and Daniel Lowney. All quotes reflect their recollections of what was said and, with the exception of Daniel Lowney who has since passed away, were reviewed by the subjects for accuracy.

Information about the charges against Donald Webb and his background came from a variety of sources. Those included author interviews with retired members of the Massachusetts State Police, Taunton police retirees and retired FBI agent Phil Torsney, as well as Jim Poydence and his three-page complaint and supporting affidavit submitted to District Judge James H. Galbreath. Additional information about Webb came from interviews with George Bates, retired New Bedford police officers as well as Massachusetts prison records and police records from Colonie, New York.

Also reviewed were articles in local newspapers, including :
"Suspect charged in death of Saxonburg Police Chief," by Mark Celender, Valley News Dispatch (PA), December 26, 1980.

Information about the New Years Eve stake out came from author interviews with George Bates, John Crede, Phil Weiner and Daniel Lowney.

Chapter 3
Two Lives Collide

Background information about Donald Webb and Lillian Webb came from a variety of sources. They include interviews with Phil Torsney, Thomas MacDonald, George Bates, Jim Poydence, Daniel Lowney and retired New Bedford police officers including Paul Boudreau, Gardner Greany and Antero Gonsalves.

Also, a wide range of public records and newspaper articles were relied on. Information about his schooling and criminal background came from articles in the *Taunton Daily Gazette, The Boston Globe* as well as the Massachusetts Department of Corrections and Colonie, New York, Police Department reports. Information about Lillian Webb's first marriage came from city and town records as well as an account in the *Standard-Times* of New Bedford, Massachusetts daily newspaper.

The records and newspaper accounts included:
Commonwealth of Massachusetts, Division of Vital Statistics. City of New Bedford. "Certificate of Marriage Record." Stanley John Portas and Lillian Carmo Correia. October 1953

Commonwealth of Massachusetts, Divison of Vital Statistics. City of New Bedford. "Certificate of Death Record," Stanley J. Portas, Jr., Feb. 28, 1956." Filed March 1, 1956.

Commonwealth of Massachusetts, Trial Court, Probate and Family Court Department. "Military Affidavit." June 17, 2005.

"Portas-Correia Nuptials Are Held." New Bedford Standard-Times, October 14, 1953.

"Ex-Tauntonian In Bank Holdup." Taunton Daily Gazette. July 1, 1955.

"Court told $5,145 Bank robbery Opposed by Holdup Defendant." The Boston Globe. September 14, 1955.

"Grove Hall Bank Holdup Case nears Suffolk Court Jury." The Boston Globe, September 16, 1955.

"Robbed Mattapan Bank Alone, Says Suspect." The Boston Globe. July 3, 1955.

The Commonwealth of Massachusetts, Division of Vital Statistics. "Certificate of Marriage." Donald Eugene Perkins and Lillian Carmo Portas "Correia." March 8, 1961.

Colonie (New York) police department complaint by Officer Mike Wildzumas, January 5, 1979.

Commonwealth of Massachusetts, Trial Court, Probate and Family Court Department. "Military Affidavit." June 17, 2005.

FBI suspect notecard copy from 1980.

Colonie Police Department and New York vs. Donald Webb, Supporting deposition by Officer Marvin Graves. January 5, 1979.

Colonie police department complaint by Officer Mike Wildzumas, January 5, 1979.

Town of Colonie and People of New York vs. Donald Webb. Deposition of Francis Truax, January 5, 1979.

Colonie Police Department and New York vs. Donald Webb, deposition of Genevieve Truax, January 5 1979.

Information about Chief Gregory Adams came from a variety of sources, including author interviews with Patricia Elsenrath, Joe Hixon, Francis Rhyskek, John Rhyshek, Colette Sullivan, Richard Sullivan, Mary Ann Adams Jones and Gordon Mainhart.

Also, Saxonburg police records and information supplied by Pennsylvania librarians and libraries were relied upon, including the information from Chief Adams' high school yearbook.

Chapter 4
Coping

Information about cleaning the Chief's cruiser came from author interviews with Gordon Mainhart, Joseph Beachem,

Chris Birckbichler and Max DeLuca

Information about Gordon Mainhart as the new Police Chief came from author interviews with Mainhart as well as newspaper articles published at the time. Those articles included:

"New Saxonburg Police Chief Experienced," by Debra Spisak, *The Butler Eagle*, January 6, 1981.

Information about the number of police officer deaths were found in the report "Death on Patrol: Felonious Homicides of American Police Officers" by the Police Foundation.

Information about Pennsylvania State Police packing up the Saxonburg office came from author interviews with John Crede, Jim Poydence, Gordon Mainhart and Sue Haggerty.

Additional information about the Adams family came from author interviews with Mary Ann Jones.

Information about law enforcement transfers and Pennsylvania troopers leaving Massachusetts came from author interviews with John Crede, George Bates.

Details about Webb placed on the FBI Most Wanted Fugitive List came from a variety of sources, including interviews with Pete McCann, Jack McGraw, George Bates, Paul Fitzgerald, Antero Gonsalves, and other law enforcement officers, FBI posters, police internal notices as well as Pennsylvania and Massachusetts newspaper articles.

The newspaper articles published in Massachusetts included:

"On FBI list.," *Herald News of Fall River*, Massachusetts, May 16, 1981.

"'Wanted' criminal seen in Fall River." *The Standard-Times* of New Bedford (MA), July 3, 1981.

Details about the discovery of the gun came from author interviews with Joseph Beachem and James Poydence

Information about law enforcement surveillance of Lillian Webb came from extensive author interviews with law enforcement officials, including Jack McGraw, George Bates, John Crede and Dan Lowney.

Information about life for the Adams family after the death of Chief Adams came from Mary Ann Adams Jones

Chapter 5
Haunted

Information about the continued search for Donald Webb and the Rhode Island meetings came from interviews with George Bates, Jim Poydence and Pete McCann. The agenda of the FBI investigative meeting in Rhode Island was also referenced.

Information about the search in Miami came from FBI official (FBI May 1982) records, George Bates and other law enforcement officials who had knowledge of that search.

Information about law enforcement interviews with members of the Fall River Gang and other Donald Webb associates, as well as sightings of Webb came from author interviews with Jim Poydence, Thomas MacDonald, Phil Torsney, George Bates, Chris Birckbichler. All quotes are based on the recollection of those interviewed.

Information about the search in Canada came from multiple interviews with Jim Poydence, Dan Lowney and Paul Carey.

Information about the new Saxonburg police department patch came from author interviews with Gordon Mainhart.

Additional details came from the original sketches and paper-work from Gordon Mainhart's personal archives

Information about the television show re-enactment of the attack on Chief Adams came from interviews with Gordon Mainhart and Danny McKnight. Additional information from news accounts of the television program was used. These articles included the May 11, 1989, story in the *Butler (PA) Eagle* by Geof Becker.

Chapter 6
Moving On

Information about efforts to find Webb and how the town of Saxonburg coped in years after the killing came from author interviews, public records and news articles.

The author interviews included those with Mary Ann Jones, George Bates, Jack McGraw, Jim Poydence, Danny McKnight, Thomas MacDonald, Phil Torsney, John Rhyshek, Melinda Berzonski, Maria Berzonski, Beau Sneddon, and Jeff Sneddon.

Information about Lillian Webb's divorce from Donald Webb came from public records filed in the Bristol County courthouse in Taunton, Massachusetts. Those records include:
Commonwealth of Massachusetts. "Legal Notice." Commonwealth of Massachusetts, February 7, 2005.
Commonwealth of Massachusetts. "The Trial Court, Probate and Family Court Department." Judgement of Divorce, Lillian C. Webb v. Donald E. Webb. June 17, 2005.

Information about the history of the FBI Most Wanted List and the agency's efforts to catch dangerous fugitives came several sources, including:
History of the FBI Most Wanted List came from FBI's Most Wanted—Incredible History Of The Innovative Pro-

gram, Madison & Adams Press, 2017, by The Federal Bureau Of Investigation.

"Oregon has starring role as FBI's most wanted list turns 60," By Bryan Denson on Oregonlive.com., published March 13, 2010.

Public Assistance Remains Crucial to Helping Catch Dangerous Fugitives, March 12, 2020, on FBI.gov.

Information about the occasional searches for Webb in Massachusetts over the years came from author interviews with Jose Gonsalves, Preston Paull, Joseph Costa, James Poydence, Jack McGraw, Fred Roberson, as well as other law enforcement officials in Pennsylvania and Massachusetts.

Chapter 7
New Look

Information about the re-opening of the case came from extensive author interviews with Phil Torsney, Noreen Gleason, Thomas MacDonald, Richard Pires, Chris Birckbichler, Dale Birckbichler and Mary Ann Adams Jones

Information on the number of unidentified persons in the United States came from National Institute Of Justice Missing Persons And Unidentified Persons: The Nation's Silent Mass Disaster By Nancy Ritter. Accessed Nov. 6, 2018

Information about entering blood samples in the case into the CODIS system came from author interviews with Chris Birckbichler

Additional information about CODIS came from:

"Federal Bureau of Investigation, Laboratory Services: Combined DNA Index System." www.fbi.gov. https://www.fbi.gov/services/laboratory/biometric-analysis/codis (accessed 2018).

"Federal Bureau of Investigation: Frequently Asked Questions on CODIS and NDIS." www.fbi.gov. https://www.fbi.gov/services/laboratory/biometric-analysis/codis/codis-and-ndis-fact-sheet.

Information about the first search of Lillian Webb's house came from information obtained in Massachusetts State Police search warrant affidavits from later searches, interviews with law enforcement officials with knowledge about the house and the later law enforcement interview with Lillian Webb at her home.

Chapter 8
Working Together

Information on how the FBI and state police investigators started working together on the case came from author interviews with Mike Cherven, Chris Birckbichler and Max DeLuca

Information about the investigation into Stanley Webb, Donald Webb's stepson, came from court records filed in Suffolk Superior Court in Boston, Massachusetts and the Massachusetts Attorney General's website.

Information about the lawsuit filed against the Webb family and serving the legal paperwork came from interviews with Tommy MacDonald, Floyd Teague, Mary Ann Jones and Jim Jones. Additional information about the lawsuit came from Pennsylvania news accounts, including:

"Discovery of secret room sparks lawsuit in decades-old homicide of Saxonburg Police Chief," by Karen Kane, Pittsburgh Post-Gazette, June 22, 2017

https://www.post-gazette.com/local/2017/06/22/donald-eugene-webb-most-wanted-fbi-Saxonburg-police-chief-gregory-adams/stories/201706250031

"Suit filed 37 years after slaying," by Tom Victoria, The Butler Eagle, June 2, 2017 http://www.butlereagle.com/apps/pbcs.dll/article?AID=/20170602/NEWS01/706029905

Information about the second search at Lillian Webb's home came from interviews with Mike Cherven, Patrick Hanley, Chris Birckbichler, Max DeLuca and Richard Goldinger. Additional information came from the search warrant obtained by the Massachusetts State Police for the search. Information about the Nutel gaming probe came from Suffolk Superior Court records and press releases from the Massachusetts Attorney General's Office.

Information about fingerprints and the history behind the science of lifting those prints came from a wide range of sources, including interviews with Kenneth Martin, and material from:

Brown, Eric W. "The Cyanoacrylate Fuming Method." National Criminal Justice Reference Service. 1990. https://www.soinc.org/sites/default/files/uploaded_files/forensics/For_supergluing.pdf (accessed 2018).

Bumbrah, Gurvinder Singh. "Cyanoacrylate fuming method for detectionof latent fingermarks: a review by Gurvinder Sing Bumbrah." Egyptian Journal of Forensic Sciences. July 18, 2017. www.ncbi.nlm.nih.gov/pmc/articles/PMC5514188

Information about negotiations with Lillian's attorney came from interviews with law enforcement and a review of the letter sent to Pennsylvania State Police by her lawyer.

Information about the Saxonburg Police Department lobby came from the author's personal observations. Additional information came from author interviews with Chief Beachem, William Gillespie and Fred Caesar.

Information about the meeting between retired Rhode Island state trooper Thomas Denniston and Rhode Island officials and FBI Agent Chris Braga came from interviews with Denniston and Braga. Denniston also supplied a typed report detailing his memory of the meeting.

Chapter 9
Answers

Information about the events leading up to the dig and as well as the dig itself came from author interviews with Tommy MacDonald, Chris Birckbichler, Max DeLuca, Mike Cherven, Patrick Hanley, Timothy Blackwell, David Mackin, William Tarbokas, Richard Pires, Joseph Beachem, Brian Canavan. Any quotes are based on the individual's recollection of what was said at the time and news video recordings from the scene.

Quotes attributed to Lillian Webb from her formal interview at the house came from her recorded interview with law enforcement. She declined, through her attorney, to be interviewed for this book. Information about why retired Rhode Island State Police Detective Thomas Denniston was at the house came from an interview with him and his typed report.

Information about those watching the search from afar came from author interviews with Mary Ann Adams Jones, Pete McCann, Thomas MacDonald, George Bates, Danny McKnight, and Jack McGraw. Any quotes are based on the individual's recollection of what was said at the time and were reviewed by them for accuracy.

Additional information from the dig as well as personal perspectives of the case came from author interviews with Taylor Cormier, Tim White, Blackwell, Thomas Quinn, William Gillespie, Joseph Beachem, and Gordon Mainhart.

Information on dog searches came from "The Cadaver Dog Handbook: Forensic Training and Tactics for the Recovery of Human Remains:
The Handbook" by Andrew Rebmann, Edward David and Marcella H. Sorg.

Information and quotes from Bristol County District Attorney Thomas Quinn at the press conference came from the video recording by WBSM radio posted on its website. https://wbsm.com/human-remains-linked-to-donald-webb-case-found-in-dartmouth-backyard/

Information from the restaurant where investigators gathered came from interviews with those who were there.

Chapter 10
Justice

Interviews with Gordon Mainhart provided the details about his waiting for official word about the identification. Author viewed his personal vehicle as well as the cell phone message he received.

Information about leaving New Bedford and canceling the murder warrant came from author interviews with Chris Birckbichler, Max DeLuca and Sue Haggerty as well as author personal observations of the Saxonburg court offices.

Chapter 11
Returning to Saxonburg

Information about the return of Saxonburg officials from Dartmouth, Massachusetts and the reaction came from author interviews with Joseph Beachem, William Gillespie, Fred Caesar, Linda Kovacik, Beau Sneddon and Jeff Sneddon.

The description of the parade came a video taken at the time and posted on YouTube. Also, photographs and other information of the parade supplied by Fred Caesar, curator of the Saxonburg Museum, were used to describe the event. Interviews with Fred Caesar also provided context to the event.

Information and quotes from the street dedication in Saxonburg came from the author's notes and personal observations of the event in Saxonburg.

Epilogue

Information from the September 2018 event at the Saxonburg police station and the Pennsylvania State Police retiree event came from interviews with Danny McKnight, Thomas MacDonald, Chris Birckbichler, Mary Ann Jones, Gordon Mainhart, Pete McCann, Joseph Beachem and Sue Haggerty.

The quote from the slain Chief's eldest son at the police station came from the article "FBI gives wanted poster to Chief," by Paula Grubbs, *The Butler Eagle,* Sept. 17, 2018.

The remarks by Danny McKnight at the 63rd Annual Banquet of Retired Pennsylvania State Police Association came from a copy of his prepared remarks.

The menu is from the banquet program.

Bibliography

Adams, Ben, interview by Maureen Boyle. (2018).

Allen, Jocelyn, interview by Maureen Boyle. (2018).

Antoszyk, Brian, interview by Maureen Boyle. (2018).

Associated Press. "Police guard slain." December 11, 1980.

—. "'Pray for me,' cries dying officer." December 6, 1980.

—. "Slain Saxonburg chief's son: 'I'm sad I never knew him'." December 5, 1985.

Bandey, Helen, and Terry Kent. "Superglue Treatment of Crime Scenes: A Trial of the Effectiveness of the Mason Vactron Superfume Process." *Police Scientific Development Branch* (Crown Office, Home Office Crime Reduction and Community Safety Group) 2018 (2003).

Bates, George, interview by Maureen Boyle. (2018, 2019, 2020).

Beachem, Joseph, interview by Maureen Boyle. (2018, 2019).

Becker, Geof. "Murder of Police Chief Re-Enacted for 'Most Wanted' Series." *Butler (PA) Eagle*, May 11, 1989.

—. "TV Network Received Many Phone Tips Following Show about Adams Murder." *Butler (PA) Eagle*, May 1989, 1989.

Berzonski, Maria, interview by Maureen Boyle. (2018).

Berzonski, Melissa, interview by Maureen Boyle. (2018).

Birckbichler, Chris, interview by Maureen Boyle. (2017, 2018, 2019).

Birckbichler, Dale, interview by Maureen Boyle. (2018, 2019).

Blackwell, Timothy, interview by Maureen Boyle. (2019).

Boston 25 News. *Boston 25 News.* July 14, 2017. https://www.boston-25news.com/news/investigation-of-1980-police-chief-slaying-leads-to-yard-dig/559139294/.

Boudreau, Paul, interview by Maureen Boyle. (2018).

Brown, Charles. "High-profile slaying refocuses attention on Saxonburg case." *Valley News Dispatch* (PA), July 24, 1987.

Brown, Curt. "Donald Webb died of a stroke, ex-wife buried his body." *Standard-Times of New Bedford*, MA, July 19, 2017.

Brown, Eric W. "The Cyanoacrylate Fuming Method." *National Criminal Justice Reference Service.* 1990. https://www.soinc.org/sites/default/files/uploaded_files/forensics/For_supergluing.pdf (accessed 2018).

Bumbrah, Gurvinder Singh. "Cyanoacrylate fuming method for detectionof latent fingermarks: a review by Gurvinder Sing Bumbrah." *Egyptian Journal of Forensic Sciences.* July 18, 2017. www.ncbi.nlm.nih.gov/pmc/articles/PMC5514188.

Butler Eagle. "Gun Used to Kill Police Chief Prime Clue in Slaying Probe." *Butler (PA) Eagle*, December 8, 1980.

—. "Handgun Found at Scene Killed Saxonburg Chief." *Butler (PA) Eagle,* December 9, 1980.

—. "Police Still Seek Owner of License Found in Saxonburg." *Butler (PA) Eagle,* December 15, 1980.

—. "Chief Adams had Good Rapport with Community." December 5, 1980.

—. "Our View: Slain chief not forgotten in Saxonburg." December 5, 1995.

Canavan, Brian, interview by Maureen Boyle. (2019).

Carey, Paul, interview by Maureen Boyle. (October 2018).

Celender, Mark. "Suspect charged in death of Saxonburg police chief." *Valley News Dispatch (PA)*, December 26, 1980.

Cherven, Michael, interview by Maureen Boyle. (2019).

Cherven, Michael F., Massachusetts State Police. "Search warrant affadavit and return." 2017.

City of New Bedford. "Certificate of Marriage Record." *Stanley John Portas and Lillian Carmo Correia.* October 1953, 1956.

Commonwealth of Massachusetts. "Legal Notice." *Commonwealth of Massachusetts,* February 7, 2005.

Commonwealth of Massachusetts Registry of Vital Records and Statistics. "Certificate of death, Donald Eugene Webb." 2017.

Commonwealth of Massachusetts. "The Trial Court, Probate and Family Court Department." *Judgement of Divorce, Lillian C. Webb v. Donald E. Webb.* June 17, 2005.

Commonwealth of Massachusetts v. Stanley Webb, Commonwealth's Statement of the Case. (Suffolk County Superior Court, August 1, 2018).

Commonwealth of Massachusetts, City of New Bedford. "Certificate of Death Record, Stanley J. Portas, Jr., Feb. 28, 1956." March 1, 1956.

Commonwealth of Massachusetts, Division of Vital Statistics. "Certificate of Marriage." *Donald Eugene Perkins and Lillian Carmo Portas "Correia."* March 8, 1961.

Commonwealth of Massachusetts, Trial Court, Probate and Family Court Department. "Military Affidavit." June 17, 2005.

Congressional Record. "H.R. 2829: Bulletproof Vest Partnership Grant Act of 1998." Congressional Record. Washington, D.C.: Congressional Record, May 12, 1998.

Cormier, Taylor, interview by Maureen Boyle. (2019).

Costa, Joseph, interview by Maureen Boyle. (2018, 2019).

Crede, John, interview by Maureen Boyle. (2018, 2019).

DeGouveia, Nelson, interview by Maureen Boyle. (2018).

DeLuca, Max, interview by Maureen Boyle. (2018, 2019).

Denniston, Thomas, interview by Maureen Boyle (2020).

Denson, Bryan. "Oregon has starring role as FBI's most wanted list turns 60." *Oregonlive.com.* March 13, 2010. https://www.oregonlive.com/news/2010/03/oregon_has_starring_role_as_fb.html (accessed March 3, 2019).

Elsenrath, Patricia, interview by Maureen Boyle. (2019, 2020).

Emergency Management Agency, Butler, PA. "Congratulatory letter to Gordon Mainhart." January 6, 1981.

Evans, J. Kenneth. "Police chief's killer gone but not forgotten." *Pittsburgh*

Post-Gazette, January 14, 1993.

Fair, Glenn, interview by Maureen Boyle. (2018, 2019).

"FBI suspect notecard copy." 1980.

FBI Memorandum and reports. Assorted dates of May 10, 1982, May 11, 1982, May 14, 1982, May 17, 1982, May 20, 1982.

Federal Bureau of Investigation. "Evidence Response Team." fbi.gov. 2018. https://www.fbi.gov/services/laboratory/forensic-response/evidence-response-team.

—. *FBI Ten Most Wanted Fugitives.* www.fbi.gov/wanted/topten/ten-most-wanted-fugitives-faq (accessed January 20, 2019).

—. *FBI's Most Wanted: Incredible History of the Innovative Program.* Madison & Adams Press, 2017.

—. "Federal Bureau of Investigation, Laboratory Services: Combined DNA Index System." *www.fbi.gov*. https://www.fbi.gov/services/laboratory/biometric-analysis/codis (accessed 2018).

—. "Federal Bureau of Investigation: Frequently Asked Questions on CODIS and NDIS." *www.fbi.gov.* https://www.fbi.gov/services/laboratory/biometric-analysis/codis/codis-and-ndis-fact-sheet.

—. "Public Assistance Remains Crucial to Helping Catch Dangerous Fugitives." Federal Bureau of Investigation. March 12, 2020. https://www.fbi.gov/news/stories/ten-most-wanted-fugitives-list-turns-70-031220 (accessed March 20, 2020).

Federal Bureau of Investigation. "Summary investigative FBI report on the death of Chief Adams." 1980.

Fitzgerald, Paul, interview by Maureen Boyle. (2018, 2019, 2020).

Freehling, Donald, interview by Maureen Boyle. (2019).

Gillespie, William, interview by Maureen Boyle. (2018, 2019).

Gleason, Noreen, interview by Maureen Boyle. (2018).

Goldinger, Richard, interview by Maureen Boyle. (2018).

Goldstein, Joseph. "Missing Child Case in SoHo, All But Closed, Was Revived by a New Agent." *The New York Times,* April 22, 2012.

Gonsalves, Antero, interview by Maureen Boyle. (2017, 2018).

Gonsalves, Jose, interview by Maureen Boyle. (2017).

Gordon Mainhart personal archives. "Teletype message from Gordon Mainhart personal archives."

Gordon, Bruce, interview by Maureen Boyle. (2018).

Graves, Marvin. "Colonie Police Department and New York vs. Donald

Webb." *Supporting deposition*. January 5, 1979.

Grubbs, Paula. "FBI gives wanted poster to chief." *Butler (PA) Eagle*, September 17, 2018.

Haggerty, Sue, interview by Maureen Boyle. (2018, 2019).

Hanley, Patrick, interview by Maureen Boyle. (2019).

Henry, Ray. "Ex-officer haunted by stepfather's past." *The Standard-Times* of New Bedford, Massachusetts, Febuary 25, 2004.

Herald News of Fall River. "On FBI list." *Herald News of Fall River*, Massachusetts, May 16, 1981.

Hixson, W. Joe, interview by Maureen Boyle. (2018).

Holland, Thomas D., and Samuel V. Connell. "The Search for and Detection of Human Remains." In *Handbook of Forensic Anthropology and Archaeology*, edited by Soren Blau and Douglas H. Ubelaker, 121-143. Walnut Creek, California: Left Coast Press Inc., 2009.

Hunt, Patrick, interview by Maureen Boyle. (2018).

Jones, Mary Ann Adams, interview by Maureen Boyle. (2018, 2019, 2020).

Kane, Karen. "Discovery of secret room sparks lawsuit in decades-old homicide of Saxonburg police chief." Pittsburgh Post-Gazette, June 22, 2017.

Klimko, Tony. "Police manhunt crosses state line." Valley News Dispatch (PA), December 6, 1980.

—. "Policeman slain in Saxonburg." *Valley News Dispatch,* December 5, 1980.

Kovacik, Linda, interview by Maureen Boyle. (2019).

Lauria, Richard, interview by Maureen Boyle. (2018).

Levin, Alan. "Pina Banishes Pro-Lowney Staff." *Standard-Times of New Bedford*, September 30, 1982.

Lowney, Daniel, interview by Maureen Boyle. (June, July 2018).

Mackin, David, interview by Maureen Boyle. (2019).

Mainhart, Gordon, interview by Maureen Boyle. (2018, 2019).

—. "Saxonburg police original patch design illustration." July 17, 1984.

Manula, Kris B. "Slain Chief Had 'Special Call,' Cabot Priest Says." Butler (PA) Eagle, December 8, 1980.

Mason, Melvin. "New law provides money for bulletproof vests." *Valley News Dispatch (PA)*, August 13, 1998.

Massachusetts Department of Correction. "Diagnostic Summary." 1976.

—. "Summary of Institutional History and Parole Summary." 1976.

Massachusetts, Commonwealth of. "Complaint for Divorce." *Lillian Webb v. Donald E. Webb*. January 10, 2005.

—. "Probate Court, name change decree." April 21, 1965.

—. "The Trial Court, Probate and Family Court Department." Divorce/Separate Support Summons by Publication. January 18, 2005.

McCann, Pete, interview by Maureen Boyle. (2018, 2019).

MacDonald, Thomas, interview by Maureen Boyle. (December 2018).

McDonough, Tim. "Saxonburg Taps Remaining Cop New Police Chief." Valley News (PA) Dispatch, January 1981.

McGraw, Jack, interview by Maureen Boyle. (2018, 2019, 2020).

McKnight, Danny, interview by Maureen Boyle. (2018, 2019).

—. "Prepared remarks for the 63rd Annual Banquet of Retired Pennsylvania State Police Association." September 2018.

New Bedford Standard-Times. "Portas-Correia Nuptials Are Held." New Bedford Standard-Times, October 14, 1953.

Office of Attorney General Maura Healey. "Four Individuals, Company Charged in Connection with Operating a Major Organized Illegal Gaming and Money Laundering Scheme." Office of Attorney General Maura Healey. 28 2018, June. https://www.mass.gov/news/four-individuals-company-charged-in-connection-with-operating-a-major-organized-illegal (accessed September 4, 2018).

O'Neill, Jack, interview by Maureen Boyle. (2018).

Paroli, Robert, interview by Maureen Boyle. (2018).

Paull, Preston, interview by Maureen Boyle. (2017).

Pennsylvania State Police. "Fugitive, Murder of a Police Officer." Pennsylvania State Police Bulletin, no. Third Quarter (1994).

Pires, Richard, interview by Maureen Boyle. (2018).

Pittsburgh Press. "Saxonburg Offers Help To Solve Chief's Slaying." Pittsburgh (PA) Press, December 6, 1980.

Police Product News. "Wanted." Police Product News, October 1982.

Poydence, James, interview by Maureen Boyle. (2018, 2019).

Quinn, Thomas, interview by Maureen Boyle. (2017).

Rebmann, Andrew, Edward David, and Marcella H. and Sorg. Cadaver Dog Handbook: Forensic Training and Tactics for the Recovery of Human Remains. Boca Raton, Florida: CRC Press, 2000.

"Recording of Lillian Webb interview with investigators at her home." July 13, 2017.

Retired Pennsylvania State Police Association. "Official program for the 63rd annual banquet." September 2018.

Rhyshek, Francis, interview by Maureen Boyle. (2018).

Rhyshek, John, interview by Maureen Boyle.

Ritter, Nancy. "National Institute of Justice Missing Persons and Unidentified Persons: The Nation's Silent Mass Disaster." National Institute of Justice. hthttps://www.nij.gov/journals/256/pages/missing-persons.aspx   tps://www.nij.gov/journals/256/pages/missing-persons.aspx (accessed November 6, 2018).

Roberson, Fred, interview by Maureen Boyle.

Roberts, Jerry. "2 years later, Saxonburg waits for justice." *Pittsburgh Post-Gazette*, December 2, 1982.

Roebling, Col. Washington A. Early History of Saxonburg . Saxonburg, Pennsylvania: Saxonburg Area Library archives, 1924.

Saxonburg, PA, 185th Anniversary morning parade. July 2017. https://www.youtube.com/watch?v=_Xyn9iUxnpU (accessed 2018).

Sneddon, Beau, interview by Maureen Boyle. (2018, 2019).

Sneddon, Jeff, interview by Maureen Boyle. (2018, 2019).

Spisak, Debra S. "Police Hall of Fame Honors Slain Saxonburg Police Chief." *Butler (PA) Eagle,* February 5, 1981.

Spisak, Debra S. "Saxonburg Pauses to Pay Tribute to Slain Police Chief Greg Adams." *Butler (PA) Eagle*, December 4, 1982.

—. "New Saxonburg Police Chief Experienced." January 6, 1981.

St. Jean, Robert, interview by Maureen Boyle. (2018).

Sullivan, Colette, interview by Maureen Boyle. (2019).

Sullivan, Richard, interview by Maureen Boyle. (2018).

Sylvia, James, interview by Maureen Boyle. (2018).

Tarbokas, William, interview by Maureen Boyle. (2019).

Taunton Daily Gazette. "Ex-Tauntonian In Bank Holdup." July 1, 1955.

Teague, Floyd, interview by Maureen Boyle. (2018).

The Boston Globe. "Court told $5,145 Bank robbery Opposed by Holdup Defendant." September 14, 1955.

—. "Grove Hall Bank Holdup Case nears Suffolk Court Jury." September 16, 1955.

—. "Robbed Mattapan Bank Alone, Says Suspect." July 3, 1955.

The Standard-Times of New Bedford. "'Wanted' criminal seen in Fall River." *The Standard-Times of New Bedford (MA)*, July 3, 1981.

Torsney, Phil, interview by Maureen Boyle. (2018, 2019).

Truax, Francis. "Town of Colonie and People of New York vs. Donald Webb." Deposition. 5 1979, January.

Truax, Genevieve. "Deposition." Colonie Police Department and New York v

Donald Webb. January 1979.

Valley News Dispatch . "Cop-killer hunt intensifies." *Valley News Dispatch (PA)*, August 17, 1984.

Valley News Dispatch. "Troopers in New Jersey checking murder lead." Valley News Dispatch, PA, December 9, 1980.

Vernet, Jennifer. "Service pays tribute to slain police chief." *Butler (PA) Eagle*, December 5, 1985.

Victoria, Tom. "Suit filed 37 years after slaying." *The Butler (PA) Eagle*, June 2, 2017.

Vido, Pat. "500 officers pay tribute to comrade." V*alley News Dispatch*, December 8, 1980.

Vido, Patricia. "In Saxonburg, they can't forget." *Valley News Dispatch (PA)*, December 2, 1985.

Wade, Chet. "450 policemen line Saxonburg street to pay respects." Pittsburgh Post-Gazette, December 8, 1980.

Wade, Chet, and Thomas J. Porter. "Saxonburg Police chief slain in lot by motorist." December 5, 1980.

Walkup, Kay. "Saxonburg Murder Suspect Has Used Many Aliases, Is Known As a Big Tipper." *Butler (MA) Eagle,* January 9, 1981.

—. "Gun Found Near Scene May Be Weapon That Killed Saxonburg Chief." *Butler (PA) Eagle*, December 5, 1980.

—. "Long-haired Man Hunted as Killer of Chief Adams." *Butler (PA) Eagle*, December 5, 1980.

—. "New Jersey Man Hunted in Slaying of Saxonburg Chief." *Butler (PA) Eagle*, December 19, 1980.

—. "Police Quiz Pal of Man Wanted in Saxonburg Chief's Slaying." *Butler (PA) Eagle*, April 5, 1983.

—. "Killer of Saxonburg chief sought." *Butler Eagle,* December 5, 1980.

—. "Saxonburg Slaying Suspect Put on FBI 'Most Wanted' List." Butler Eagle, May 5, 1981.

—. "Long Blue Line of Officers Pay Tribute to Chief." December 8, 1980.

—. "Police Need Break to Nab Chief's Killer." September 22, 1981.

—. "Saxonburg Murder Probe HQ Transferred to PSP Barracks." January 6, 1981.

Ward, Bob, interview by Maureen Boyle. (2018).

Weatherunderground. *Wunderground*. (accessed December 2018).

"Web conference agenda, July 14-15." July 14-15, 1983.

Weiner, Edward, interview by Maureen Boyle. (2019).

Weiner, Phil, interview by Maureen. (2019).

White, Tim, interview by Maureen Boyle. (2018).

—. *Authorities Digging in Dartmouth for Clues in Pennsylvania Murder.* July 13, 2017. https://www.youtube.com/watch?v=u1BSv700TOc.

Wildzumas, Mike. "Colonie police department complaint." January 5, 1979.

WPRI-12, Rhode Island. WPRI. July 14, 2017. https://www.youtube.com/watch?v=CItoldRCHzo (accessed January 2019).

Yamashita, Brian, et al. *The Fingerprint Sourcebook, Chapter 7: Latent Print Development.* https://www.ncjrs.gov/pdffiles1/nij/225327.pdf (accessed 2018).

Yoezle, Alida, interview by Maureen Boyle. (2018).

Photo Gallery

Photo Courtesy of Community Library of Allegheny Valley

A fresh-faced Gregory Adams in his high school yearbook photo.

Photo Courtesy of Mary Ann Jones

A happy family: Gregory and Mary Ann Adams with their two sons.

Photo Courtesy of the Saxonburg Museum

Gregory Adams as a young patrol officer, posing with then-Chief James Grady in 1976.

Photo Courtesy of the Saxonburg Museum

In uniform, Gregory Adams is shown here near the start of his law enforcement career.

Photo Courtesy of the Saxonburg Museum

Chief Greg Adams rose through the ranks to become Chief.

Photo Courtesy of John C. Rhyshek

A smiling Chief Adams in town talking with some local youngsters.

Photo Courtesy of the Saxonburg Museum

Saxonburg Police Chief Gregory Adams' cruiser with his tie on the trunk after the killing.

The Butler Eagle Photo Courtesy of the Community Library of Allegheny Valley

Investigators at the scene of Gregory Adams' murder.

Photo Courtesy of the Butler Eagle

The front page of the Butler Eagle when the Chief was killed.

AIDED WOUNDED OFFICER — Mrs. Midge Freehling and her son Don "Tiger" Freehling were first on the scene after Saxonburg Police Chief Gregory Adams was beaten and shot Thursday by an unidentified man who apparently had been pulled over for a traffic violation. Tiger told police he heard at least 10 shots which came in two bursts. The Freehlings live two houses north of the Agway parking lot on Butler Street in Saxonburg where Adams' abandoned police car was discovered. (Story on Page One.)

— Butler Eagle photo

Photo Courtesy of the Butler Eagle

PROCESSION OF MOURNERS — A grim-faced Saxonburg mayor, Reldon W. Cooper, second from left, flanked by former Saxonburg Police Chief James S. Grady, left, and Saxonburg policeman Gordon Mainhart, right, trod rain-soaked Main Street in Saxonburg on Sunday afternoon. The Saxonburg officials led a long line of enforcement officers who gathered to pay tribute to a slain policeman, Chief Gregory B. Adams. The police chief died of a gunshot wound Thursday afternoon while making a "routine" traffic stop. Heading the marchers is veteran special police officer Credo Paulsen of Saxonburg.
— Butler Eagle photo

Photo Courtesy of the Butler Eagle

FUNERAL RITES AT CABOT — Flanked by a color guard from Saxonburg American Legion Post 683 and the Sarver Veterans of Foreign Wars, Clinton Township policeman Howard Kinney, left, and Buffalo Township policeman Jon Ianotti, right, help carry the casket of Gregory Adams into St. Joseph Catholic Church at Cabot on Monday morning.
— Butler Eagle photo

Photo Courtesy of the Butler Eagle

BEREAVED FAMILY — Mary Ann Adams, the widow of Saxonburg Police Chief Gregory Adams, and his mother, Mrs. Benjamin L. Adams, are es- corted into St. Joseph Catholic Church in Cabot, where funeral services for the slain officer were held this morning. (Story on Page One.)

— Butler Eagle photo

Photo Courtesy of the Butler Eagle

SCOURING MURDER LEADS — These members of the investigating team seeking the killer of Saxonburg Police Chief Gregory Adams sift through some of the hundreds of bits of information channeled through the State Police Command Post in the Saxonburg Borough Building. The command post telephones are answered around the clock as police continue to pursue all leads in the brutal slaying of Adams last Thursday. — Butler Eagle photo

Photo Courtesy of the Butler Eagle

Photo Courtesy of the FBI

Donald Webb's 1976 NY State
Department of Corrections photo at the
Clinton Correctional Facility.

Photos Courtesy of the FBI

Headshots of low-level mobster Donald Webb.

Photos Courtesy of the FBI

Webb wearing a pink shirt while relaxing on vacation sometime before the murder.

Photos Courtesy of the FBI

Webb with wife, Lillian at left. An earlier FBI photo at right.

WANTED

BY THE FBI

Unlawful Flight to Avoid Prosecution - Murder; Attempted Burglary

DONALD EUGENE WEBB

Photograph
taken in 1979

Age-enhanced
Photograph

Aliases: A. D. Baker, Donald Eugene Perkins, Donald Eugene Pierce, John S. Portas, Stanley John Portas, Bev Webb, Eugene Bevlin Webb, Eugene Donald Webb, Stanley Webb

DESCRIPTION

Date(s) of Birth Used:	July 14, 1931; July 14, 1928	**Hair:**	Gray/Brown
Place of Birth:	Oklahoma City, Oklahoma	**Eyes:**	Brown
Height:	5'9"	**Sex:**	Male
Weight:	165 pounds	**Race:**	White
NCIC:	W346078551	**Nationality:**	American

Occupations: Butcher, Car Salesman, Jewelry Salesman, Real Estate Salesman, Restaurant Manager, Vending Machine Repairman

Scars and Marks: Webb may have a small scar on his right cheek and his right forearm. He may have the following tattoos: "DON" on the web of his right hand and "ANN" on his chest.

Remarks: Webb, who is considered to be a career criminal and master of assumed identities, specializes in the burglary of jewelry stores. He is reportedly allergic to penicillin, a lover of dogs, a flashy dresser, and a big tipper.

CAUTION

Donald Eugene Webb is being sought in connection with the murder of the police chief in Saxonburg, Pennsylvania. On December 4, 1980, the chief was shot twice at close range after being brutally beaten about the head and face with a blunt instrument. He was charged with unlawful flight to avoid prosecution and a federal arrest warrant was issued for Webb on December 31, 1980.

REWARD

The FBI is offering a reward of up to $100,000 for information leading to the whereabouts of, or the location of the remains of, Donald Eugene Webb.

SHOULD BE CONSIDERED ARMED AND DANGEROUS

If you have any information concerning this person, please contact your local FBI office or the nearest American Embassy or Consulate.

Photo Courtesy of the FBI

An age-enhanced photo of Donald Webb is displayed on this version of the FBI's Most Wanted poster.

Photo Courtesy of the Fall River Herald

This article appeared in the *Fall River Herald* months after the murder.

Photo Courtesy of Kevin Kalunian

Jim Poydence, one of the original Pennsylvania State Police investigators on the murder case.

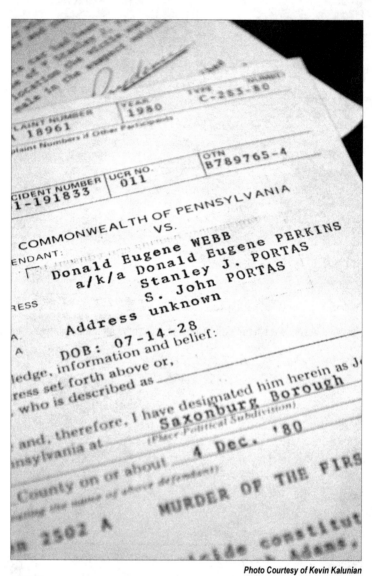

COMPLAINT NUMBER 18961
YEAR 1980
TYPE C-283-80

INCIDENT NUMBER 1-191833
UCR NO. 011
OTN B789765-4

COMMONWEALTH OF PENNSYLVANIA
VS.

DEFENDANT:
Donald Eugene WEBB
a/k/a Donald Eugene PERKINS
Stanley J. PORTAS
S. John PORTAS
ADDRESS
Address unknown

DOB: 07-14-28

...ledge, information and belief:
...ress set forth above or,
...who is described as _____

...and, therefore, I have designated him herein as J...
...nsylvania at Saxonburg Borough (Place Political Subdivision)

...County on or about 4 Dec. '80

MURDER OF THE FIRS...

...n 2502 A

Photo Courtesy of Kevin Kalunian

As shown on the cover, a close-up image of the arrest warrant for Donald Webb.

Photo Courtesy of Kevin Kalunian

John Crede, one of the original Pennsylvania State Police investigators who traveled to Massachusetts in the early hunt for Webb.

Photo Courtesy of Kevin Kalunian

The road scene where gun was discovered.

Photo Courtesy of Kevin Kalunian

Retired Pennsylvania State Police investigator Danny McKnight who worked on the case originally.

Photo Courtesy of Kevin Kalunian

Glenn Fair, the firefighter who was driving the ambulance the day Chief Adams was fatally wounded.

Photo Courtesy of Kevin Kalunian

Pennsylvania State Police Investigator Chris Birckbichler.

Photo Courtesy of Kevin Kalunian

Retired FBI agent Pete McCann.

Photo Courtesy of Kevin Kalunian

Pennsylvania State Police investigator Max DeLuca in his office.

Photo Courtesy of Bob Ward

Spot behind Lillian Webb's home in Dartmouth, Massachusetts where Donald Webb's remains were found as a dog looks on.

Photo Courtesy of Timothy Blackwell

Klaas, the Massachusetts State Police K-9, used in the search.

Photo Courtesy of Kevin Kalunian

A couple of the shovels used to unearth Webb were given to the Saxonburg Police Department.

Photo Courtesy of Taylor Cormier

The Saxonburg Police Chief's cruiser and the Massachusetts Crime Scene unit at the Dartmouth home the day of the dig.

Photo Courtesy of Taylor Cormier

Massachusetts State Police Sgt. William Tarbokas (center), who helped unearth the remains, shown in the driveway of the Dartmouth house. Tarbokas was assigned to the State Police Crime Scene Services.

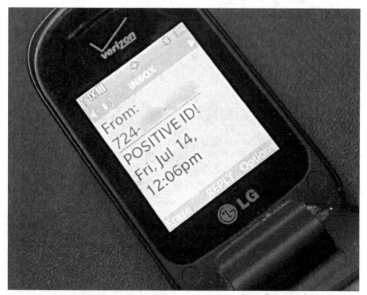

Photo Courtesy of Kevin Kalunian

Text to retired Saxonburg Police Chief Gordon Mainhart confirming the identification of the remains as Donald Webb.

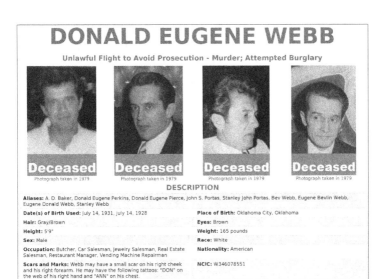

DONALD EUGENE WEBB

Unlawful Flight to Avoid Prosecution - Murder; Attempted Burglary

Deceased — Photograph taken in 1979

Deceased — Photograph taken in 1979

Deceased — Photograph taken in 1979

Deceased — Photograph taken in 1979

DESCRIPTION

Aliases: A. D. Baker, Donald Eugene Perkins, Donald Eugene Pierce, John S. Portas, Stanley John Portas, Bev Webb, Eugene Bevlin Webb, Eugene Donald Webb, Stanley Webb

Date(s) of Birth Used: July 14, 1931, July 14, 1928

Hair: Gray/Brown

Height: 5'9"

Sex: Male

Occupation: Butcher, Car Salesman, Jewelry Salesman, Real Estate Salesman, Restaurant Manager, Vending Machine Repairman

Scars and Marks: Webb may have a small scar on his right cheek and his right forearm. He may have the following tattoos: "DON" on the web of his right hand and "ANN" on his chest.

Place of Birth: Oklahoma City, Oklahoma

Eyes: Brown

Weight: 165 pounds

Race: White

Nationality: American

NCIC: W346078551

Photo Courtesy of the FBI

Once Donald Webb was found, the FBI issued this wanted poster proclaiming him deceased.

Photo Courtesy of Erica Dietz

This Saxonburg cruiser was parked outside Lillian Webb's home as the remains were exhumed, then led and closed the town parade.

Photo Courtesy of Kristen M. Setera

Tommy MacDonald and Phil Torsney, two of the many FBI agents who worked on the case.

Photo Courtesy of Danny McKnight

Chris Birckbichler, one of the Pennsylvania State Police investigators on the case, introduces Tommy MacDonald (left) and Danny McKnight (center) at the retirees' dinner in 2018.

Photo Courtesy of Danny McKnight

The Birckbichler family at the Pennsylvania State Police Retirees' Dinner in 2018 with FBI agent Tommy MacDonald. (L-R) Dale Birckbichler, Chris's dad; Gloria Birckbichler (Chris' wife); Pennsylvania State Police Sgt. Chris Birckbichler; Flo Birckbichler (Dale's wife) and FBI Special Agent Tommy MacDonald. The senior Birckbichler was on duty the day of the Chief's homicide.

Photo Courtesy of Danny McKnight

Two of the investigators who helped close the case and two who were there at the start gathered at the Pennsylvania State Police retirees dinner in 2018. (L-R) Chris Birckbichler, retired FBI agent Pete McCann, FBI agent Tommy MacDonald and retired Pennsylvania State Police investigator Jim Poydence.

Photo Courtesy of Kevin Kalunian

Ben Adams, Chief Adams' eldest son, and retired chief Gordon Mainhart hold the street sign during the dedication ceremonies renaming a section of a street in honor of the slain chief.

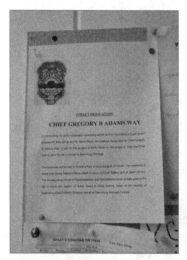 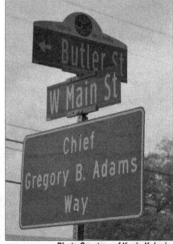

Photo Courtesy of Kevin Kalunian

Left: Notice posted in downtown Saxonburg announcing the street dedication for Chief Gregory B. Adams Way Right: The section of Butler Street where the chief was killed was renamed in 2018 Chief Gregory B. Adams Way.

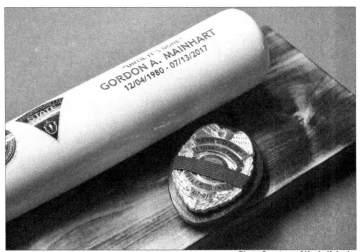

Photo Courtesy of Kevin Kalunian

The memorial bat given to retired Saxonburg Chief Gordon Mainhart, who had his mounted. FBI agent Tommy MacDonald presented police involved in the case similar bats.

Photo Courtesy of Kevin Kalunian

Close-up of the bat given to those involved in the case. Saxonburg Chief Joseph Beachem is holding the one he was presented.

Photos Courtesy of Kevin Kalunian

A commemorative coin given to investigators in the case sits atop former-Chief Gordon Mainhart's scrapbook (top). Front and back views (bottom).

Photo Courtesy of Maureen Boyle

The case file containing the arrest warrant for Donald Webb at the Saxonburg Courthouse.

Photo Courtesy of Kevin Kalunian

Fred Caesar, head of the Saxonburg Museum, shows a display.

Photo Courtesy of Kevin Kalunian

Author Maureen Boyle with Fred Caesar of the Saxonburg Museum, and Saxonburg Police Chief Joseph Beachem, look over some files in Saxonburg's downtown.

Photo Courtesy of Kevin Kalunian

Display at the Saxonburg Museum featuring the wanted posters for Donald Webb.

Photo Courtesy of Kevin Kalunian

Judge Sue Haggerty holds the original arrest warrants for Donald Webb.

Photo Courtesy of Kevin Kalunian

Judge Sue Haggerty holding a copy of the H.R. 2829 Bulletproof Vest Partnership Grant Act of 1998.

Photo Courtesy of Kevin Kalunian

Where the Chief was killed, as it looks today.

Photo Courtesy of Kevin Kalunian

Author Maureen Boyle with Chief Joseph Beachem visiting where the gun was found.

Photo Courtesy of Kevin Kalunian

Memorial for Police Chief Adams outside the Saxonburg Municipal Center.

Photo Courtesy of Kevin Kalunian

To this day, a photo of Chief Adams hangs in the lobby of the Saxonburg Police Department.

Photo Courtesy of Kevin Kalunian

Chief Gregory Adams' grave.

CPSIA information can be obtained
at www.ICGtesting.com
Printed in the USA
LVHW082105150723
752419LV00003B/225

9 781934 912966